Women in America

FROM COLONIAL TIMES TO THE 20TH CENTURY

Women in America

FROM COLONIAL TIMES TO THE 20TH CENTURY

Advisory Editors
LEON STEIN
ANNETTE K. BAXTER

A Note About This Volume

The upsurge of trade unionism in the early New Deal years gave new impetus to workers' education and revived the liaison that had developed earlier in the century between working women and a group of women's colleges. Especially noteworthy were the Bryn Mawr Summer School for Working Women, the School for Workers in Industry at the University of Wisconsin and the Vineyard Shore Workers School on the Hudson in New York State. Joined as the Affiliated Schools for Workers, they reached out to working women in the garment shops, textile plants and retail stores and brought them to summer sessions, institutes, weekends and formal classes. There they were taught history and economics, were trained in leadership and strengthened in their own resolves by group discussions of personal histories. This scrapbook gathers a sampling of their autobiographical accounts, written while in attendance at one of the Affiliated schools. They are unadorned reports of strikes, exploitation, organizing efforts, work with men, and confrontations with bosses.

I Am a Woman Worker

Edited by

ANDRIA TAYLOR HOURWICH

and

GLADYS L. PALMER

ARNO PRESS
A New York Times Company
NEW YORK – 1974

Reprint Edition 1974 by Arno Press Inc.

Reprinted from a copy in
  The University of Illinois Library

WOMEN IN AMERICA
From Colonial Times to the 20th Century
ISBN for complete set: 0-405-06070-X
See last pages of this volume for titles.

Manufactured in the United States of America

———◆———

Library of Congress Cataloging in Publication Data

Hourwich, Andria Taylor, ed.
  I am a woman worker.

  (Women in America: from colonial times to the 20th
century)
  Selected autobiographies from Affiliated schools
scrapbooks.
  Reprint of the 1936 ed. published by the Affiliated
Schools for Workers, New York.
  1. Women--Employment. 2. Women in trade-unions--
United States. I. Palmer, Gladys Louise, joint ed.
II. Affiliated schools scrapbook. III. Title.
IV. Series.
HD6053.H67 1974   331.4'092'2 [B]   74-3954
ISBN 0-405-06102-1 . . . .

I AM A WOMAN WORKER
- A Scrapbook of Autobiographies -

Edited by

Andria Taylor Hourwich
and
Gladys L. Palmer

Published by
The Affiliated Schools for Workers, Inc.
302 East 35th Street
New York City

FOREWORD

A valuable by-product has grown out of the Summer Schools for Workers - the incentive to speak and to write. This expression is not the polished word of the advanced student. Workers are far too busy and engrossed in their daily industrial lives to worry about every phrase, every comma, even every climax. They live, and they feel. Many of them, fortunately, can write their stories for other workers, and the very simplicity of the tales is climactic.

Several years ago, a group at the Bryn Mawr Summer School was studying trade union problems. The members of the group described orally their own industrial experiences. Soon they began to put their stories on paper, with the help of both their economics and English teachers. Some accounts were first hand experiences with union and strike activities; some dealt with labor history; some were reviews of books on the labor movement. But all the articles were written by and for workers.

Out of these efforts grew what was called the first Scrapbook of the American Labor Movement, published by the Affiliated Schools for Workers. Since then several new Scrapbooks have been issued - each one meeting with such success that the editions were soon exhausted. The present volume, I Am A Woman Worker, varies from its predecessors in that the material is not restricted to one class within one school. These are selected stories from various workers' schools.

Such a collection has more than an informational value. One of the purposes of publishing this pamphlet is to show local groups how they too may develop a similar record of their own individual and group activities. Every worker has a story to tell, and most workers can with some encouragement and assistance put their experiences on paper. Such a process points up valuable happenings, and out of a collection of those a basis for group action may be formulated.

Perhaps some day we will have a much more comprehensive record, embracing more activities and more industries, and including contributions from men as well as women. The labor movement needs this record of its rank and file members. Until then, we hope I Am A Woman Worker will be of interest and help.

Andria Taylor Hourwich

TABLE OF CONTENTS

INTRODUCTION

The stories told here form an important item in the raw material of workers' education. Economists tell us that they are not economics: they contain for the most part neither statistics nor generalizations from the statistics. In the ideas of old fashioned English teachers, some of the accounts are perhaps not English - at least as it is taught in old fashioned schools - though to a prejudiced view the English in these stories is infinitely preferable.

These stories have been basically inspired by economics teachers as a part of the workers' education way of learning economics. Whatever English teachers have done to help to inspire them has been effected chiefly by playing ball with the workers' education process. The stories tell from the point of view of the workers themselves "what happened to me." The writing created and vivified for them usually for the first time in their lives the idea that "what happened to me" is important. It is interesting to others; it is a part of history.

It has been my privilege, as one of the English teachers associated with one of the economists in this program, to have had a part in helping to fan this flame of enthusiasm and to increase the confidence of some of the authors of these stories in the significance of their experiences and the worth whileness of telling them. These are accounts that teachers, literati, comfortable white collar people, can never tell. To me they are well told here. Moreover, the telling of them did most significantly fulfill an important educational function. The groups of fine, experienced women, in which the stories were told and shared, learned how to use the exciting "wake each other up" technique.

After all, it is this "wake each other up" experience, and the vital learning that follows it, that is the high point in the lives of all those teachers and students who love education.

William Mann Fincke
Director, The Manumit School

GETTING A JOB

LOOKING FOR A JOB

An early morning – a cold, rainy morning. A narrow street. Filthy lunch-wagons, little dark oyster kitchens, stores with all kinds of rubbish in them, moving picture houses with pictures of half-naked girls and cowboys on horseback, with a sign in front of the entrance: "10¢ Any Seat, Any Time 10¢."

Among all this, a door with a charcoal sign on a piece of cardboard is hardly noticeable. "Operators on dresses wanted, 3rd fl.," says the sign.

Will there ever be an end to the steep, muddy stairway? For a moment a shiver passes down my back. Something stirs in the darkness, and the eyes catch a glimpse of a large gray rat coming slowly down the steps.

The first impulse is to run back, far from the stairway, away from this street. But the magic sign, "Operators wanted, 3rd fl.," forces me to go on and on.

How many more steps are there? Thirteen ... fifteen ... nineteen ... Here is the door. How do you open it?

Inside. There is a row of machines, twenty or so. Little lamps are attached over each one, so low that they light up only a pair of hands and cast a faint reflection upon girls' faces, leaving the rest of the room in darkness. Motionless are the faces of the women; motionless are the aching, bent backs. It seems that only arms and hands live in this place. Not a glance is passed among them, not a word. Only the dynamo is burning endlessly, interrupted now and then by the rattling machines that come like rushing waves and suddenly quiet again.

One more machine will run today; one more place in the row will be occupied!

A CITY EMPLOYMENT OFFICE

After Christmas I am usually a lady of leisure; by this I mean there is no work in my place, and not being able to get along on meager savings for long I am compelled to look for temporary employment.

While on one of these missions, I walked slowly down some street absorbed in my own thoughts. I was very exhausted after another vain search. Suddenly, I was startled by a strange crying voice. I woke up from my dreams and looked around in the direction from where the voice came. I noticed a sign Employment Bureau, and I heard the voice coming from there.

Since this was just the place I had in mind to look up, I entered. I saw a tall slim girl with a pale face in shabby clothes, and her hair somewhat in disorder crying in a loud pleading voice: "It is nine months since I am out of work, I have a sick mother to support, we are starving, I must have a job." The woman behind the desk jumped up in fury, her face was scarlet and her eyes sparkled with a green light like a cat's on a dark night. She shouted at her in a squeaky voice: "Now listen there, girlie, I have heard enough of those hard luck stories. Why don't you shine your shoes and put on some decent clothes. This is no place for vagabonds." Saying this she walked out closing the door in front of the poor victim's nose. The girl walked out sobbing as though her heart was going to break. I followed her with tears rolling down my cheeks, thinking: "Gosh, what a miserable world this is, something must be done."

AN EMPLOYMENT AGENCY

Men and women, young and old, colored and white, fill the chairs or remain standing in the large, dismal stuffy room. Noise and chatter come from all corners. Partitioned off by an iron screen sits the manager at her desk. Every now and then her voice rings out, "Quiet, please!" The chatter and the noise go on.

Suddenly the telephone rings. Silence! Everyone's attention is fixed on the desk at which the manager sits. She gets up, comes into the center of the room, looks round, goes over to one of the young women and whispers something. The young woman gets up, goes to the desk, gets a slip of paper from the manager, and walks out, a smile on her face. Everybody's eyes escort her to the door with envy.

An hour passes. She comes back looking sad and disappointed. She goes up to the manager and says something in a whisper.

"But you don't look Jewish. I thought you'd get by," we hear the manager say.

The telephone rings again. Again silence.

"Is anyone of you men a college graduate?" asks the manager.

"I am - what's the job?" eagerly answers one of the young men.

"Pushing a truck," is the reply.

"What are the wages?"

"Twelve dollars if you are good."

"And I went to college for this!" he says with bitterness in his voice. But he adds quickly, "Yes, I'll take it."

MY FIRST JOB

With my heart pounding against my ribs as if it would suffocate me, I approached the girl at the desk. In vain did I strive to find my voice. It was as if some power held it back. With one motion I extended the newspaper and pointed to the advertisement which read: "Girl Wanted."

"Up one flight, the door on the right." High and sharp came her voice as she tried to talk above the metallic click of the typewriters.

Slowly I climbed the stairs; on the door the sign read Cutting Department. As I entered it seemed to me the noise was absolutely deafening. On one side of the room were huge machines of iron. These machines swing up and down, looking as if they would devour the men that stood before them swinging their slightly bent bodies back and forth, back and forth, while they pressed the pedals that controlled the giant machines.

The floor was littered with little half moons of leather. White leather, brown leather, black leather. Girls too were sitting at long benches, hopelessness in every move of their hands, dejection in every move of their bodies. It was then as I beheld them that a feeling of dismay gripped me. Would I become one of these?

A FIFTH AVENUE DRESSMAKING SHOP

Our boat made a record time in October, 1927, five days from Cherbourg to New York. I was very anxious to see my father and brothers whom I had not seen for years. On the boat we made a plan with my mother in America that she should cook for us and I would clean the house and go to school while father and the boys would work. When we arrived my father took us down from the boat. When we got home in our five room flat, all my dreams were gone. I said to my mother that I could not sit at home and go to school when I saw my father and my brothers working so hard and not making even a fairly comfortable living for us. My mother started to cry. She felt that she could not let me go to work and travel alone, a kid like me. (The fact is that in Europe we were not allowed to go alone on the street.) I tried to think what kind of work could I do, and came to the conclusion that I knew nothing. I was very dis-spirited and asked my relatives to give me an idea of what trade to learn. They told me just to look for a job, and I would be shown what to do.

One of my cousins took me to a neckwear place to learn how to make ties, because this was known as a good trade. I struggled four weeks on neckties, and made just a few dollars a week. I hated so much to work at this trade that I went out to look for another job, but I was either afraid or ashamed to go into the shops and come out without anything. But very good news was waiting for me. A friend of mine needed a finisher in the place where she was working, a union place where they had a forty hour, five day week. She promised me she would show me everything. I was so happy and excited that I could not sleep all night, and in the morning at 6:00 was all ready to go to the place which was not open until 8:00. There my friend told me that she would give me light work to do, so that they should not see that I was not ex-perienced. Otherwise I might have been sent away; they are not allowed even by union to do it the first week.

The dresses that we were working on were selling from $250 up. They had even $1000 dresses and I was afraid even to work on them, but I had to because of the forelady's being happy that she had a chance to watch and bother someone. She was watch-ing me all the time and made me so nervous that by the end of the week I had lost a few pounds. On Friday, the fitter who took charge of our department came to see how I was working before they made me a permanent worker in the shop. She said she was satis-fied with my work. When I punched my card at 5:00 and saw the other card for next week, I could have screamed for happiness be-cause I did not have to struggle to find a job any more.

Then, when I got acquainted with the girls, they told me

stories about our customers. One of them ordered in one season
so very many dresses that at the very end of the season they had
to design a few more models specially for her even though we had
fifty or more different styles and she had ordered in some styles
three or four different shades, too. This lady was a wife of a
broker in Wall Street; and when her husband went into bankruptcy
her bill for a season was $10,000 which she could not pay.

The president of one of the biggest electric power holding companies has three daughters and a wife. They are our customers, and every season they spend about $25,000 for dresses from my
shop. Each daughter has her own car and chauffeur. Sometimes when
one of them makes up her mind that she wants a particular dress, we
have to rush out the dress in one day because the poor girl had nothing to wear. We are continually working for them, and making
every week for each one three or four dresses.

But our trade is breaking down slowly, like all the others,
because these customers who used to order twelve dresses at an order
now only take six at a time. Those who ordered only one or two, do
not order now at all.

Our boss does not seem to feel it as bad as we workers do.
She still has her four to five carat diamond rings and other jewelry,
and a Rolls-Royce car, with her chauffour waiting for her all day.

THE GLOVE FACTORY

When I graduated from grammar school, my first thought was to get a job. One of my sister graduates was already working in a glove factory. When she promised to take me to the employment office, I was so excited, I ran all the way home yelling before I got to the stairway, "Mama!" My mother thought something had happened and she ran to the door, scared. When I could collect my thoughts I told her Mollie was going to get me a job. She laughed at me and told me that I was still a child, that I had better go to school because nobody would employ me anyway. But I would not listen.

The next morning I was up before sunrise for fear I should not be ready on time. At last a quarter of seven arrived. As I was approaching the meeting place I stopped short, my heart began to beat fast. Is it possible that I am late? Could my friend have been there and left? I wanted to hide and cry. As I turned to leave I heard a voice calling my name. I turned around, there was my friend running to meet me.

At last we were on the train. My friend sat down but I would not, for fear I should miss the station.

When we got to the factory my friend showed me the employment office and left me there. I walked in very timidly and sat down besides a row of other applicants. When my turn came to be interviewed I became confused, but the woman in charge encouraged me a great deal. First I was put through a physical examination, which I passed. Then I was sent to another room. By now I had picked up courage and answered all questions enthusiastically.

I told her that I liked to work and I would be very conscientious. "That's what all the young girls say at first, then they become lazy," she told me. But I promised I should be different.

Finally I was taken to a large room, lit up by artificial light. In front of each girl was a steaming machine. The dampness crept into one's bones. The forelady showed me how to work. I envied her as I would a magician, how easily she handled the dummies, I was even afraid to try. After a period of struggle, I got my hand into it.

Within a few days, I became ill from all the dampness and noise and had to be absent for a few days. When I came for my pay the bookkeeper coaxed me to return. Two weeks later I was put on piece work. Now I began to compete with the older help. The first week I received $13, which was $3 more than the straight work. This thrilled me so that I tried to make more the next week.

Suddenly the examiner began to return my work because I would either tear the gloves or else not steam them enough. That discouraged me, so that I began to lose interest in my work.

When visitors came through the factory, the forelady would get up to talk to them. I saw no reason why I should not at least look at them, and when I did I was reprimanded. This was the climax. I continued to work for six weeks longer, then I quit. No amount of coaxing and inducements could change my mind. I later learned that due to the terrible conditions of the factory they could not keep girls long enough for them to become thoroughly experienced. They therefore picked them young and foolish.

MY FIRST DAY IN THE MILL

Early one Saturday morning about 6:50, a group of girls stood at the entrance of a hosiery mill. A middle-aged man was talking to them one by one. When he got to me, he asked my name and then introduced me to a young fellow, the inspector. "Have you room for another rider girl?" "No," was his reply. "Well, then, put her to folding." I followed the inspector through the mill, by rows and rows of girls. He finally stopped at a friendly looking girl about three years older than I. He introduced us and said to her that she was to teach me how to fold.

The girl told me to go to the other side of a table. She explained the work she was doing. There were several marks on the table. I was told to fold the hose by two of these and given a box to measure to see if I was getting them just right. When this work was finished, she went to a nearby desk and put her name down. A man came and brought another truck of work and put one size on the table. The girl then explained the traveller to me. It is a sheet of paper which comes with the work telling just how it should be folded and the kind of bands to use. I heard a loud hissing sound. "What's that?" I asked. E. explained that when a girl wanted some work put on her table she hissed for a boy to come and do it for her. "Don't ever let Mr. B. see you lift more than ten dozen," E. said. "Why?" I asked, for ten dozen of hose are not heavy. She explained that the boys were hired to do such work, and Mr. B. did not think the girls should lift heavy things.

I had developed a headache and E. said we could go up-stairs and get something for it. We went through a rest room where a colored woman was washing the basins and on to the nurse's room. There were several beds all made up neatly, and a nurse in a starched uniform at her desk. She was nice to me, and we went on back to work.

This time we were putting the hose into envelopes. E. said she guessed I was tired since I was not used to standing all day, and suggested that I sit down and put the flaps of the envelopes inside as she folded them. I hesitated because everyone else was standing. "It will be perfectly all right. Don't be afraid, no one will say anything to you," she said. So I sat down for a while. Several of the girls stopped their work and came over to ask if I was sick.

During lunch time I made friends with several girls. The bell rang and we went back to work again. In a little while, Mr. B. came around and filled out an insurance blank for me. He asked me how I was getting along. "Who is that gray-haired man over there?" I asked. "He's the superintendent of the finishing department," E. said. She went on to say that he was very nice and that I need not feel uneasy when he was around.

The bell rang and the day was over. E. and I walked out together. At the corner she turned with a gay "See you Monday." I walked home thinking of my day's work. It had been a pleasure because everyone had been so nice and friendly. It was not at all as I had pictured a mill. Somehow I thought in a mill people worked from morning till night without stopping, just like machines.

I GO TO WORK

At the age of fifteen, I started work in the twisting department of the R. Mill, a branch of a large woolen company. The first morning I reported to work, after I had taken off my hat and coat, I stood around talking to some of the girls I knew. All of a sudden out of the stillness of the room a loud shriek was heard which resounded throughout the mill and seemed to be right in the room. To my surprise I soon discovered it was the whistle outside on top of one of the roofs. After this loud shrieking had stopped, the girls I had been talking to all seemed to scatter in different parts of the room leaving me standing there alone in a quandary, not knowing what to do.

As the girls started their machines in operation, the room became a mixture of different noises. The hum of machines and the shrieking of the belts on the pulleys which keep the shafts overhead in motion so the girls can run their machines, seemed to form a throbbing sensation through my head and vibrated throughout my whole body.

As I stood watching all the different wheels turning this way and that, looking like a jig-saw to me, the foreman, a short stocky Englishman, came walking up the room. To my surprise before he spoke to me, he seemed to look at me with a funny twinkle in his eyes, as if amused at knowing that I was just about scared to death watching the girls placing their hands on different parts of these monster-like machines which are in motion from 7:00 until 5:00, stopping only for lunch hour. He introduced me to one of the girls and told her to teach me how to run a twisting machine.

The girl did her best trying to teach me how to run these machines, but I was so frightened I didn't even want to touch them. The machines really frightened me so much that the girl who was teaching me told the foreman that I was too young to do this work and too small a child to be put on them. The girls working on these machines were all around the age of thirty.

The foreman then placed me on the Foster winding machines. This was a simple job and I soon learned to run these machines very efficiently. This work was on a piece-work basis and I averaged between $20 and $25 a week for full-time work. I had not been working on these machines very long when one of the yarn carriers for the twisting machines gave up her work to return to school, and as the foreman thought I would like this sort of work I was moved again. This was about the easiest work I ever did, and the most interesting to me because, while working on this job, I could roam all over the plant talking to girls I knew who were working in different departments. Of course this work did not pay as much as the Foster winding but I didn't have to work so hard. This job was a standard job and paid $17.50 a week.

I continued working at the job for about a year when the
time clerk took suddenly sick. At this time I was studying a business course, and the forelady knew this. She told the foreman to
let me take over the time clerk's work until she was able to return
to work again. Not knowing the forelady had told the foreman to
put me on this job, I was astounded when he came up to me and told
me to come to work in the morning prepared to take over the clerical
work.

Not expecting the regular time clerk to be sick for a very
long time, I worked for about four weeks at my regular yarn carriers
pay. The fifth week the foreman was looking over the payroll and
told me the regular clerk would be out quite a while and that I was
to receive a regular time clerk's pay. This was a salaried job paying $27.50 a week. I held this job until the company started clos-
ing up their plants. This plant was one of the first to be closed.

MY DAYS AS A LEARNER

For days and days I hunted for work. Days fled into weeks, and weeks into months, and still I was looking for work. Ten cent stores, restaurants, cafes, mills, mills, mills — and all said "No, we can't use learners. Too many experienced hands already. Had to lay off ——." I got to the point where I hated every day that came, for with every new day came a renewed search for work. I looked for work in nearby cities. No luck — so back I came.

At last a friend told me to go to work with her, and she would show me how to weave and I could apply as an experienced hand in the future.

Bong, clong, clammer! I never heard such noise as I entered the weave room door. People rushed to an fro, starting looms, tying threads — and the noise! My friend spoke to me but I was deaf with the roar and I followed her dumbly.

She shouted at the foreman and asked him if he would let me stay and learn to weave. He shouted back that I could if somebody would agree to teach me. A man over in the farthest corner of the room promised to let me work with him beginning on the following Monday for six weeks.

Monday I got up at 5:00 A.M., drank a cup of coffee, ate an egg and a biscuit and left for work. I had to walk a half a mile and catch a bus at the highway. I ran most of the way through the woods for fear of missing my bus, and too, I was a little afraid of the darkness — even though I had a flashlight.

I waited by the roadside. Two workers passed me on their way to the silk mill. A light appeared in a window on the opposite side of the road. I smelled meat frying. "Fat back and gravy," I thought. Something rustled in a cornfield nearby and a dog came trotting past. Two or three cars whizzed by, another and another — other workers hurrying to work; other slaves like me, only they got paid for being slaves — not much, but some. My toes were frozen.

Then came the bus, with great headlights, and around the edge red and green ones. I waved frantically for him to stop. I got on and searched with numb fingers for my 25 cents and bought four bus tokens. The bus driver smiled. "A little chilly, eh?"

As day was breaking we alighted at the mill gates and once again I entered into the weave room. My fingers were clumsy. I broke threads and my teacher patiently helped me and showed me what to do. And every few minutes the bossman and foreman would come around and watch me.

I began to think about quitting time. I was dead tired; my back ached from stooping and tying those everlasting threads. I went to look at the clock. It was 11:00, and we worked until 3:00 P.M. The weave room was hot and stuffy.

I watched the other workers. Like bees, they worked — running, walking, stooping, starting looms, stopping looms — endlessly the eight hours through. Never speaking to their neighbors, seldom looking up, they smiled sometimes.

My "teacher" pointed out a dried-up looking man in the center isle with a gun on his knee. "That's a stool pigeon," he said. "Keep away from him."

That very day after work, the stool pigeon came to me and was very friendly. I left him alone.

That night I had dreams of the mill; of the grinning stool pigeon; of the soured-up foreman; and of looms — looms and cloth.

I had worked two weeks before I had a "smash up" which kept two people busy for the rest of the day tying string together. The next day it happened again and I was afraid to touch the looms. I was so tired and nervous, I cried. My teacher was, of course, losing by my mistakes, but he was very nice and did not fuss. "Everybody does that when they're learning," he said, and after work, on my way home, he told me funny stories about how he used to make mistakes and the sly way he got by with it. I felt much better.

After five weeks, I did not mind the roar so much. I could hear very easily. Then they put me on six looms by myself and told me I would get pay. I went home that day triumphantly. The foreman gave me eight looms very soon and it kept me running every minute of the eight hours I worked. I hated it — everything about it. On my first pay day I drew $9.

Then they began cutting work down. I got three days a week. A month passed. I got cut to two days. Another month and fourteen of us were laid off at once. And then I was again in the great army of unemployed.

I BECOME A HOSIERY TOPPER

I started to learn topping in the hosiery trade in 1919 when I was eighteen years old. I had worked in various trades and industries up to that time for I started to work at the age of fourteen. None of the mills I worked in were organized and my pay varied from $3 to $12 per week depending on trade conditions and my age. The last job I had was at seamless hosiery looping. I lost this for taking part in political activities and voicing my opinions. After looking for work at various seamless hosiery mills and getting the same reply, when they found out my name, I realized that I must be blacklisted in that particular trade, so the only thing for me to do was to learn something new.

I started out to try my luck in finding employment in the full-fashioned hosiery mills. When I came to the hosiery mill district, there was one mill with three companies in the one building. After finding enough courage, I went in to apply for a job. The first and second company offices I could not find. I tried the third and there I got a job as a learner on topping.

After learning six weeks, the superintendent placed me on a steady job, a thirty-three gauge, eighteen section machine, making heavy weight silk stockings. We also had a helper and the toppers filled nine bars each and loose coursed their own work. At first I only filled six bars and another learner helped me out until I acquired the speed to fill and loose course all my work which took a couple of weeks longer. I received $10 per week while learning and afterwards was paid piece work which amounted to $20 and $1 from the knitter for helping at the machine. How happy I was when I was bringing home over $20 per week.

The men were organized in this shop. The girls were not organized; the men considered it too much trouble, and were afraid the girls would demand too much.

After I had worked in this shop for a year, my knitter lost his job as he was working on a sick job and the other knitter returned from the sanitarium. In the meantime my first knitter got a job at the N. and L. Hosiery mill. He asked me to come and work for him there, as it was a new job on a Reading machine - thirty-nine gauge, twenty section silk half hose, and a $23 guarantee until I made more, and with no helper; I would get $2 extra for helping on the machine. I worked there six months when my knitter got discharged for not turning out production. The boss said he would not start that machine up again as he did not have any orders for it. This shop was organized 100 per cent and we also had a shop association. The girls paid 10 cents a week beside their monthly dues to the union, to which I also belonged. When I lost my job at N. and L. I was really too stupid to tell the chairman of the shop committee about my grievance, but accepted the fact that I was out of a job and could not do anything about it.

After a period, I got a job topping on lace ingrain at N. N.'s. The topping was different because it was the English style foot. It did not take me long to learn this new type of topping, and I was soon earning between $35 and $40 per week. This was 1922 and the knitters in the shop were organized. The girls were not organized in this shop, but as toppers were scarce in this new style of work, we generally received our demands. About the same time they introduced lace stockings in other shops in the city. The C. Shop where my sister was employed had a difficult time getting toppers to do this type of work, so she persuaded me to come and work with her which I finally did.

Most of the plain gum silk jobs were working short time. In our shop, these workers had practically all the summer of 1923 off. Only those operating new style of lace machines were kept working. The knitter, for whom we were working, made good money and saved. He invested in property and later went in business with his brother who was a legger in the same shop. The two brothers and father and an outsider opened up their own mill. They started with one set of machines consisting of one footer and two leggers which would run two shifts. My sister and I went to work for this knitter; we were the first girls in that new shop. I worked through six years, with intervals of summer vacations and trips, and when I would return I always received employment again. We were 100 per cent organized and received high wages for this plain service weight gun silk stocking. We averaged from $40 to $50 per week; around $50 per week when working overtime, for we received time and half. The gauge of the machine was thirty-nine and twenty section. About the time I left the shop, they had six footers and twelve leggers, twelve toppers, six loopers, eight seamers, and they also finished their own work. This shop would not sign up with the union in the 1929 agreement, and the hosiery workers went out on strike against wage reductions, in February, 1931. The workers lost the strike and the shop is now working only part time with scabs and old union workers.

When I left this shop in 1929, I went back to work in the C. Shop. Conditions were not the same as previously. The wages were already dropping. My average for a full week was $32 and $1 for helping at the machine. I worked at the C. until the following summer when I left for a camp and travel. When I returned I could not find employment and was out of work for over a year except for three weeks when I worked on a temporary six hour night shift. When the general strike of the unorganized shops occurred, I did voluntary picketing.

I got a job in August, 1931 at the Z. hosiery mill. Here I did mesh topping, for none of the girls were willing to work on it. It was a Reading machine, forty-five gauge, twenty-four section, each topper filling twelve bars and loose coursing her work. This shop had been out on strike in the spring of 1931, and the union had organized it. The job was night shift, 3:00 P.M. in the afternoon until 1:00 A.M. at night. The shop was on the fifth floor and it was as hot as a steam oven. The German knitter I was working for would close the window when he had trouble with operating the machine. (What a stupid idea!) I worked three weeks when

I was laid off until the new agreement would come into effect. In
October, I was called back to work and worked part time up to a
couple of weeks before Christmas. In the spring we formed a shop
association so the manufacturer would live up to the agreement.
When the shop association was organized with a representative of
each department on the committee some of the workers thought the
committee could perform miracles over night.

After Easter the firm moved some of the machines to a town
in a nearby state, as the town had invited them. They let them have
a building free of charge and taxes free for ten years providing they
hired and taught the town people the trade. Wages there are lower
than in our city.

SOLDERING

I reported for work at 8:00 in the morning. While I was waiting for the foreman to place me, the conveyor started. The place began to get smoky. I heard shouts, "Up! the belt!" "Down! the belt!" Radios were turned on, radios were turned off. On and off, off and on! It was driving me mad. Suddenly the boss called me.

"Can you solder?"

"No."

"All right, I'll teach you," he said, and he handed me a soldering iron.

I felt the weight of it; "I can't hold it," I thought.

Then he gave me a piece of solder. "Watch me," he said, as he soldered two sets, four lugs on each.

"Can you do it?" he asked.

I answered half-frightened, "I'll try." I soldered one set.

He looked at it and said, "Not so bad, try another."

After I had done another set, "Okay," he said. "Now try just two lugs instead of the whole operation."

I soldered for about an hour. Then I began to get dizzy. It was the moving of the conveyor, and the inhaling of acid fumes. The place was a cloud of smoke. My wrist got weak. It felt as though it was breaking from the weight of the iron. I could not hold the iron steady. It slipped and burnt my fingers. My solder got caught in the plug from my iron and blew out the fuse. This made a terrible noise. Hot sparks flew from it. I could control myself no longer. I began to scream.

"Oh, I can't stand this, I can't." I was in great pain. My wrist felt as though it was broken. My fingers I had burnt were still stinging, and I had a large blister on one. My neck was stiff from bending over the conveyor. I ached all over. I began to cry; but I finally did learn the job.

COTTON MILL WORKER

When I first started to school, although I was only seven years old, my one desire was to finish High School and become a nurse. That was not asking much, but even that was denied me. For during my seventh year in school, my father was taken sick with lung trouble which was caused, the doctors said, by working too hard in a cotton mill where there is so much lint and dust. It was a long time before my father was able to be up, and then the doctor told him he must not go back to work at the same place, if he wanted to live. The wages then were a little more than a cotton mill worker gets now, but even that wasn't enough.

If you will notice very closely, you will find that ninety-nine out of every hundred cotton mill workers have a pale, delicate look caused by long hours and the unhealthy conditions they work under.

School was out the first of June, and so I started to work in a hosiery mill the 8th of July, thinking I could start back to school the coming session. But my father's income was so low I was compelled to keep working so my two small brothers and one sister could stay in school. Many girls have been forced to give up their desires and ambitions in order to help support their families, because of conditions their parents had to work under.

What we must fight for now is shorter hours and more pay in order to keep our health and be a help to the coming generation.

THE SYMBOLIC JACKET

What ever I knew of styles in dressing was from an old fashioned book dated before the war, which I found in our small town dressmaker's work room in Russia. The dresses we wore were made out of sack, old sheets, or table cloths that did not need much style. It was not a question of style but of how to cover one's body in those days.

The leather jacket that came with the Revolution, was to me a symbol both of Revolution and elegance. My admiration for the jacket I brought with me to America, and made sure to get one as soon as possible.

But my desired leather jacket brought me a lot of trouble after I had lost my first job and was looking for another one.

I answered an ad in the paper. It was a dressmaking shop. The man came to the door, who was short and stout, and had a big cigar in his mouth. With one glance at me, he burst out in a hoarse voice, "Can't use you," and slammed the door in front of my nose.

Next came a jewelry box factory. After waiting for one hour in the hall, I was admitted to an office where a tall handsome young man with a heavy cigar in his mouth (a sign of big business) was sitting behind a large mahogany desk with an air of dignity. He politely invited me to sit down and the questioning began.

"What is a union shop?"

"I don't know what you mean," I answered, although I had, in fact, belonged to a union for two years.

"Don't you belong to a union?"

"No."

"You know I don't like it when someone else wants to run my business."

"Oh! I understand that."

"What is your name and address?"

I told him, and he answered, "Come in tomorrow."

But tomorrow another man came out, I presume the foreman; he asked my name and disappeared. In a few minutes he came out again and the answer was, "I'm sorry, Miss, the place is taken; come in some other time."

Then I applied as a learner in a millinery shop. The forelady, who engaged the girls, said to me, "I am sorry, Miss, we don't like Bolsheviks."

"What makes you think I am one?"

"Never mind, I can see it at once. These leather jackets and bushy hair, I know them well."

Later I got a job in a men's clothing shop. After I had worked there a few weeks, the boss showed a tendency to familiarity towards me. He promised to give me a lesson in behavior. For that he got the coat in his face, and I quit the job. The reason for such behavior was again my leather jacket which made him think I was a Communist.

For a year I heard the words "I can't use you." "Not to-day." "Taken." "Come some other time." I got sick and tired of it, and decided to get rid of my Jacket. I dressed myself in the latest fashion, with lipstick in addition, although it was so hard to use at first that I blushed, felt foolish, and thought myself vulgar. But I got a job.

This occurred some years ago. Now, however, there is no more danger in wearing a jacket. It does not signify radicalism, because the American student took to wearing it.

LIFE IN THE FACTORY

ONE DAY OF LABOR

Six-forty-five A.M. How quiet it is in this place where thousands of workers bend their backs in hard monotonous toil, for the monster that drives the machinery still sleeps. How footsteps and voices carry through the silent rooms with their thousands of stilled belts, pulleys and millions of spindles.

But soon the silence is broken; the monster stirs. Trembling and quaking, the building groans as if in protest against the tremendous power within its walls. With a bellow to be heard for miles, the voice of the factory commands the arms and legs of the machinery to start work. Workers reluctantly slide levers and press buttons. Pulleys turn slowly, then gain speed. Belts hiss through close, hot air. Bobbins on their spindles revolve faster than eyes can see. The monster is awake, demanding, driving, compelling. On! On! On!

Night time is near. Hours of labor have passed in a perpetual grind. Heat! Mist! Dust! Work! All in a mad, endless whirl. Clothes wet with perspiration and the clammy thick mist from the hissing humidifiers. Dust, clinging and irritating. Work, hard work, sapping strength from the strongest, leaving the weak gasping. Tired eyes lift from their minute tasks to send swift glances at the slow-moving clock, but hands and arms continue without pause. Weariness, the vanguard of swift death, has spared none.

At last, the lights flicker and die. The voice has again bellowed, but this time unheard because of the clank and hum of tireless machines. With a last burst of speed, their tenders slam levers back; belts and pulleys halt reluctantly. With feet that feel like lead, the workers carry aching bodies through the now silent rooms. Free at last to leave. Free to rest as much as trembling bodies permit. It is the end of one day.

ON THE OTHER SIDE OF THE DOOR

As I stepped into the office, the door behind me came to
with a muffled thud. I felt it hit my foot. My first glance at the
room in front of me, so amazed me that I stopped still.

Straight ahead of me was a long corridor. The floor was
covered with a dark green carpet. On the right was a partition like
in a bank. On the left was a private office, closed with frosted
glass. The name of the owner of the mill was in large gold letters
on the door. On down the hall past the boss's office were four or
five steps leading down to the street entrance. The green carpet
covered the steps like a brook, running over moss-covered rocks. On
either side of the steps were brass rails, gleaming from the reflection of the lights which hung by brass chains from the spotless
plastered ceiling. Beyond the wire were twenty-five or thirty stenog-
raphers, all smartly dressed. They looked very efficient and well-
bred. They seemed to blend with the cream colored walls, and the rich
mahogany finish of the chairs, desks and the two settees which were
straight in front of me.

I listened. How strange - I could not hear the monotonous
throbs of the machines. Then I remembered the heavy thud I had felt
on my heels just a few seconds before. All I heard now was the steady
tap-tapping of the typewriters and adding machines.

I walked over to the pay roll department which was the first
window to the right and asked for the money that was to be advanced to
me out of my last week's check. I had got a leave of absence from my
job for several weeks. The paymaster did not ask my name. He asked
my clock number. The bills were counted through the window. I
thanked him and retraced my steps to the door. I took hold of the
glass knob that was set on the mahogany colored door, pushed it open
and stepped back into the hall of the mill. I turned and looked back,
the spring on the door had already pulled it shut. What I saw was a
door painted a dull gray set off by a worn tin door knob.

Again I heard the throbs of the machines and the yells of
the lot boys. Through a door on down the hall, I caught a glimpse
of girls bent over machines, their dresses, smocks and aprons blended
with the drab gray of the walls and ceiling. The door of the first
aid room opened. A girl came out, crossed in front of me and went
out of sight through the door. The index finger of her left hand was
bandaged. I wondered if girls would ever stop running machine needles
through their fingers. I turned and walked down the four or five steps
to the street entrance. There was no green carpet here and no brass
rail to slide my hand along. I stepped out the door and walked up the
street, wondering why the hell I had thanked the man when the money he
gave me was mine. And besides that I had had to go to the employment
office to get a signed permit to go beyond the sacred portals.

THE BOSS

He enters the factory bringing with him an atmosphere of untiring activity. His worst victim is the shipping clerk.

"Louie! What are you doing?"

"I'm - eh, I'm - eh -"

"All right - get through with it!"

The next minute he's at the blockers. "Who made this hat?"

The forelady approaches. "Is there anything wrong with it?"

"Isn't there? Does it look perfect?"

Forelady: "It looks all right to me."

"Is it just like the sample? Get the sample, get the sample." Impatiently - "Now listen! If the girl can't make it right give it to someone else."

"I don't see anything wrong with the hat; it looks all right to me."

"Now listen, I'm running this business. Do you want me to stay in business? If the hats will keep on coming out this way, I'm going to stop making hats altogether." As usual he has the last word.

"Louie! Get away from the girls. Look how you handle the hats. Watch out, you big dope!"

A spry little man about 5 feet 4 inches tall, always doing something, even too busy to take off his hat and jacket on the warmest days.

"Miss Bee, trim up those brim hats right away." The next minute he's discussing business with his partner.

Now he's near the cutter. "Did you get the material? Is it all right? Order fifty more yards."

Now he's pressing. The chairlady is asking him to settle prices. "Just a minute, just a minute."

"When will you come in?" she insists.

"In a minute. Wait - in a minute. Louie, did you ship Baer's order?"

"I'm packing it now."

"Hurry up. Don't get lost."

"Mr. T. . . . .," the chairlady calls impatiently.

"All right - I'm coming. Louie, come here. Press those crowns and don't watch the girls."

In an out, here and there, sometimes the eye is too slow to follow his movement. Sh! The boss is out, disappeared as fast as he appeared, and the hurry and bustle disappears with him.

A ROMANTIC REALIST

"I've one more tie to go, I've one more tie to go." Over and over I hummed this to myself. It was a grand game, those first days at the neckwear factory. I would sing at my work then.

Pick up a bundle, untie the string, turn the ends, inside out, inside out, press it down, turn the ends, inside out, press it down, turn the ends......

Rhythm and song and color, those first days. Blue ties, red ties, yellow ties, dotted and spotted, plaided and striped. Romance in ties. Wonder who will wear this one? Will he be thin, fat, a banker, a truck driver, kind, cross, hard-boiled, sentimental - perhaps someone I know, or a stranger miles away?

But something happened to the game. It is no longer fun. Rhythm has changed to monotony. Colors are all drab now. Just got another cut in salary. That's 40 per cent now, and no work at all yesterday. I haven't time to wonder about design and color, no time to rhapsodize; just get this bundle done, turn, press and fold it. Then race like mad to the forelady, get another bundle (if the order is still unfilled) and start all over again.

I think of that coat that I can not have if we get another cut; and the girls are whispering about a lay-off. Mother has that big coal bill to pay before she can order any more. And I promised the kid nephew a pair of boxing gloves this pay day. Guess I will have to break my promise; these shoes of mine need repairing so badly.

I feel so tired now, even if there is only half as much work. Work cut down, salary cut down, and the forelady cross as a bear. I can't believe that this is the job I once thought such fun. Fun! Racking your brain to find a way to make 50 cents stretch into a dollar! Fun! Almost working your fingers off so you'll be "next" on the waiting list! Fun! Staring a lay-off in the face while you watch the boss ride home with his chauffeur!

I wonder if the "big shot" sings at his work? We have taken a number of salary cuts, but his salary doesn't seem to have suffered. Wonder if his coal bin is empty, and if the bill collectors hound him to death. I wonder if his kid is heart-broken because he is refused a 20 cent pair of boxing gloves.

MY CLOTHING SHOP

At 8:00 A.M., thirty minutes late, I slide into place at my machine ignoring the sarcastic comments from all the girls.

"Good afternoon," says a masculine voice nearby, and I look up into the foreman's face. "Why did you bother to come in at all?"

To this I say nothing but a polite, "Good afternoon." He then proceeds to pile work beside the machine, by turns scolding me for being so late and pleading with me to hurry the work out. Other girls keep coming in until after 8:30. Then the whole shop settles down to a busy day. The foreman is everywhere giving out work and fighting because the work is going out bad.

Suddenly voices are raised above the machinery. Red, the girl on the machine next to me, is fighting with a smaller girl for taking all the easy work. Immediately the boss comes over and yells at both of them and divides the work. After he goes on the girls continue to insult each other. Some take sides; others remain neutral.

The machinist, angered by insistent calls from several girls to fix their machines, picks on one girl and shouts, "Damn you, what did you break it for?"

"I didn't break it on purpose. I can't help it if the crazy thing won't work," she answers.

"Hell you can't," and he keeps on cursing at the top of his lungs, while the girl, young and new in the shop, runs into the ladies' room, a dirty little closet in the side of the wall, to cry. Then the bell rings and girls troop out, laughing and arguing, to punch a time clock and eat.

Late again. This time I got in unnoticed for the foreman is giving work to the pressers. Poor kids, their job is no cinch in this hot weather. The heavy steam flats seem to weigh a ton and perspiration drips from them freely as the boss hurries them in their work. Very often these girls work until 7:00 and 8:00 at night, and during the noon hour too. The afternoon wears on with the usual quarreling, singing, and the hum of voices above the drone of the machinery.

Suddenly all is quiet. The smell of cigar smoke is strong upon the air. This smell is a warning that the owner of the shop is near. You can always smell him before you see him. Presently he enters, a tall well-built man with slightly graying hair. He walks up and down past the girls, who are working swiftly now. No one talks except when spoken to by the boss.

He picks up garments, inspecting each one separately and closely, looking for bad work. Everyone holds her breath for fear it is her work he is looking at. If he finds work that is poor, his temper explodes, and we have an exciting half hour. Then he stalks out swearing to shut up the place immediately. When you can no longer see or smell him, the atmosphere changes. Voices again buzz excitedly all over, and keep up until 5:30, when the bell rings and the girls slowly and wearily depart, calling good night to each other.

A SEAMER ON MEN'S UNDERWEAR

I am seventeen years old, but look to be fifteen or younger. When I was twelve, I was hurt by an automobile. Because of the injuries I received, I could not go to school. That was a bitter blow, not only to me but also to my parents. They had worked hard in factories so that I could get an education. At the time of the accident, my mother was working in a cotton mill. Being tired and over-worked, the terrible shock of my accident caused her to have a nervous breakdown. She could not work. The few hundred dollars that they had saved, dwindled to nothing. I know this, and worried.

So, at the age of fourteen, I went to work. The doctor who took care of me said that I was in no condition to work, and if I did I would pay for it in a few years. Because I had no training in any kind of work, I always got jobs that were the most monotonous and the poorest paid. I finally got work in a knitting factory as a seamer.

This is my daily program.

At 5:30 it is time for me to get up. I am tired and sleepy. After I got up, I hurriedly eat my breakfast, and I am ready to go to work. It is a chilly winter morning, but I know that it will be hot in the mill. I start on my three mile walk to the factory. As I walk, I see others hurrying to work. I look at the older people and wonder if they, too, feel the resentment every morning that I do, or if as the years go by their spirits are deadened.

I arrive at the factory. The sight that I dread to see meets my eyes: the line of unemployed people waiting for the boss to come and hoping for work.

As I open the door, a force of hot stuffy air greets me. I rush to my machine, as all the girls do, to get ready, so that when the whistle blows we can start working. When doing piece work, every minute counts.

I seam men's heavy underwear. After I finish twelve union suits, I get a check for 6 cents for size fifty, and $4\frac{1}{2}$ cents for the smaller sizes. At the end of the week, I paste my checks in a book and give the book to the boss, who pays according to the number of checks I have. After I finish a dozen union suits, I tie them up and carry them to the bin. The dozens are heavy, and grow heavier as the day goes on. The bin is usually full, and as I throw my dozen up on top it very often comes down on me. Of course I fall. Rupture is quite common from carrying the heavy dozens.

One woman who has worked in this mill for seven years is home now with a rupture and a strained back. She cannot do her own housework. A girl of eighteen came to this mill from high school. She got the same job that I am doing. In one of the processes of seaming, you start and stop the machine with your foot. The motion is very jerky. This girl, not used to hard work, strained her legs through this motion. Now, she can not walk without a cane. The city doctor - she could not afford a specialist - can not cure her. Now, at the age of nineteen, she leads the life of a recluse, alone, bitter and hating life. Only last year she was an eager, healthy child, loving life, and having wonderful plans for the future. There are many like this woman and this girl and myself who are seaming men's underwear.

Nothing much has happened today. My machine has broken twice, and because the machinist has not been very busy, I have had to wait only about three-quarters of an hour. After my many trips to the bin for my work, and after finishing each dozen, tying it up, signing my number on the check, then carrying it to the next bin, I am so tired that my body and mind grow numb. To arouse myself, I go to the ladies' room. The toilet does not flush very well, but it never does anyway. When I come to the water fountain, no matter how tired and numb I may feel, I am always angry and disgusted. The water is lukewarm; the fountain is rusty and filthy. But my trip to the fountain serves as a stimulant because I am always glad to get back to by bench.

As usual, half of my lunch has been spoiled. I can either put it on the table where I keep my work and where it becomes squashed, or I can put it in a box under my bench and give the rats the first choice.

After a monotonous afternoon, it is almost time to go home. We have three minutes to put our coats on; then we wait in our respective aisles. All eyes are on the boss, waiting for the signal. Then we rush out. This race track scene is part of the working day. When I come out, a force of fresh air meets me, the air that I have been longing for all day. My subconscious mind is aware of this, but I am so tired that I only feel my aching bones and my tired eyes.

As I walk home, I see some of the people for whom my class works. The priest rolls by in his big car, and gently nods his head to me. The superintendent's daughter waits in her car for her father. I think of my father who has to stay one more hour in the mill, then trudge home where his daughter will be too tired to greet him.

As I think of those things, there is a terrible rage in my heart, but I do not stop with that. I want to learn what crushes out the lives of workers, and what takes the children of these people and places them in the stuffy factories, even before they have time to fill their lungs with fresh air.

A NECKWEAR SHOP

The factory is a partitioned half of the show room cut a-
cross vertically. On entering one is struck with the roar of the
machines and the dingy, dilapidated room. A stranger would have a
tendency to stoop over, for fear of touching the extremely low ceiling. This is due to the necessity of more space so the balcony was
added to the already crowded dungeon. This is only one of the names
we have for the hated work-shop.

The tables containing the machines are set out in rows.
When more machine space was needed to keep up with the demand, parts
of each table were sawed off hardly leaving enough elbow room. While
working the girls would very often poke each other and without a
"pardon me" would again resume the steady grind.

The right hand side of one of the machines is actually hugging a post placed there to support the newly constructed balcony.
The girl working at this machine is fortunate enough in being left-
handed, so the post does not interfere with her arm. We often told
her to mark that defect to one of her assets. The machines are con-
gested, she does not have the needed room to put her work boxes, and
she must stop at frequent intervals to get her work. On making a
complaint, the employer said, "I'll have a shelf made." We all know
this statement to be ridiculous, for a girl can not be getting up
momentarily to reach on a shelf for work, especially when it is piece
work.

The hand workers sit in the rear of the shop almost hugging
two garbage cans, from where the nauseating odor of stale lunch left-
overs most always fill the air. When there is a sudden calamity of
girls rushing forward, making one think of a land rush, we know that
the barrels are being emptied making the atmosphere unendurable.
They rush closer to the window until the filth is carried out. There
is quite a supply by the time the barrels are emptied, for it costs
money to have them taken out. The boss does not think business is
good enough to have them taken out too often.

My seat had been in the center. Here, too, the air was
suffocating, and I looked for an opportunity to change for a seat
near the window. A vacancy occurred, though it was very unfortunate
for someone. (A girl was fired. The boss complained about her work
but we all know it was for other reasons. During a recent strike in
the trade she was very active.) I took her seat near the window.
Here the air is plentiful but it is not so pleasant when it comes in
full force making my back quite stiff. I have thought of going back
to my original seat, but it is a choice between the cold or stale air.
I choose the former.

Here we work the entire day illuminated by Edison's grand invention, the incandescent lamp. It is quite convenient in the winter when our fingers are too stiff from the frost, for we warm them by holding our hands close to the bulb for a few moments. In the summer, however, we shut the lights off at intervals to try and escape the intense heat.

There is an opening in the office which looks into the workshop. Here the employer can sit concealed for hours listening to the complaining going on between the workers, and watching us at work at our daily, monotonous task.

MY SHOP

The shop that I am employed in is situated on the highest floor of a building in a large eastern city. It is an extremely large place which is kept clean and sanitary. My boss is a manufacturer who specializes in producing women's fine silk undergarments.

It is two years now that I have been working here as an operator, and in spite of the fact that the shop is not an organized one it has fairly good conditions. We work forty-four hours during a five day week and are being paid for holidays, and also time and a half for extra hours. There are a hundred girls working steadily throughout the year, and only during the Christmas season when we are piled with work are more helpers hired.

My boss happens to be a woman who is wise enough to know how to run her business quite well. She is our forelady as well as our boss giving out the work and keeping track of what we produce during the day. That means that we are constantly rushed with our work, because each girl tries her utmost to beat the one sitting next to her.

When slack time comes, and there is less work, we find ourselves in a much worse predicament. If a girl has to wait a few minutes until work is given to her, then the boss comes over with hatred in her eyes and says, "All right, that's nice, sit this way even till tomorrow. I am losing money on this order and you are sitting there with your hands folded. The only reason I took this work is because I don't want you girls to stay at home."

One day I was working on a special order of gowns and I found some sleeves missing. I called the boss over and explained to her the situation. She flared up and said, "Missing, impossible. I myself counted the sleeves before it was given to you. I don't understand what you did with them." This time I could not control my anger, and told her that I was not a thief, and that if I were to take something I would take a thing which would be more useful to me. I went to the dressing room thinking that tomorrow I would have to look for another job. Just then my boss called me back and asked me in a pleasant voice to sit down near the machine. She brought over a new bundle of work, and explained how it was to be done. Later I asked the forelady, about those sleeves and she told me they were found lying on the cutters' table. Since then my boss has more confidence in me, and therefore I am being treated in a much better manner.

A TYPICAL WORKING DAY OF A COTTON MILL SPINNER

I work in a cotton mill as a spinner, and receive $21 a week for 48 hours of work.

I arrive at the mill about 6:45 to begin work. Our actual starting time is 7:00, but we always start five minutes before then.

In this factory, the speed-up system is in full sway. I used to tend ten sides; now I tend twenty lengthened sides (other spinners with short sides tend thirty). Each side has 126 ends which makes 2,520 ends to watch, and every end I must supply with roving. The roving runs out every four days, while the ends break very irregularly all the time. I generally piece up about three ends a minute. The work that I do covers four alleys of frames about 300 feet long. Just how often I walk around them, I do not know - without question, numberless times.

Before I was placed on the added number of sides, I used to tend ten sides at which I pieced up the ends that broke down, cleaned the frames and the rollers, under which the ends run, and did my own creeling (that is, I put my own roving in the creels).

During that time I noticed strange men with stop watches in their hands. They were watching every motion of the workers, making notes of everything that happened. Everything was checked: time out for a drink of water, visits to the toilet, even if a worker spoke to another. The result was that machinery was placed where it would reduce the amount of walking by a spinner; gears were changed to speed up the machines; half the spinners were laid off, and those who remained were given twice as much work as well as piecing up and passing the board - a form of cleaning that takes about fifteen minutes to do and has to be done every hour. The remaining work - cleaning and creeling - was now done by two workers, who were poorly paid. This speed-up system has created unemployment, and has placed a terrible strain on the workers' nerves.

In the spinning room, as in all parts of the mill, the workers are in a hurry, running here and running there. They rush to the toilet, rush for a drink of water, and rush while working. The irony of it all is this: safety posters on the walls read, "If you run, you'll fall down on your job. Ask yourself what's the hurry?"

During my working hours, I constantly dodge trucks in narrow aisles, and unguarded belts and pulleys. The floors are washed while the machinery is running; slips and falls occur. Often while stripping thread or roving of bobbins, the hand is cut, or slivers pierce the skin. But the most dangerous thing is that slow but sure occupational disease, tuberculosis, which lurks in all textile mills. Deaths resulting from tuberculosis are extremely numerous. Is it any wonder? The rooms are cold in some spots, and hot in others; where the humidifiers are, it is damp. Also, we constantly breathe cotton dust.

SOUTHERN MILL HANDS

When I moved from the North to the South in my search for
work, I entered a mill village to work in a cotton mill as a spinner.
There I worked eleven hours a day, five and a half days a week, for
$7 a week. In a northern mill I had done the same kind of work for
$22 a week and less hours. I worked terribly hard. My boss was a
farmer who knew nothing about regulating the machines. I had not been
there long when he was fired, and an overseer from the North with his
speed-up and efficiency system was hired in his place. I do not know
which was worse: to work under a man who did not know how to make the
work run well but who was pleasant to work with, or to have well regu-
lated machines which ran better but a driving boss.

The sanitary conditions were ghastly. When I desired a drink
of water, I had to dip my cup into a pail of water that had been brought
into the mill from a spring in the fields. It tasted terrible to me.
Often I saw lint from the cotton in the room floating on top of the lukewarm water. All of the men chewed tobacco, and most of the women used
snuff. Little imagination is needed to judge the condition of the
water which I had to drink, for working in that close, hot spinning room
made me thirsty. Toilet facilities were provided three stories down in
the basement of the mill in a room without any ventilation. Nowhere was
there any running water. Even in the houses provided by the company
there was no running water.

The married women of the South work extremely hard. The majority of them work in the mill besides having large families to care
for. They arise about 5:00 to take the cow out to the pasture, to do
some weeding in the garden, and to have hot cakes ready for their hus-
bands' breakfasts when they arise. Then they prepare their children
for school, and finally start their work in the mills at 6:30 where
they work for eleven hours. Upon their return to their homes, they
have housework to do. They have no conveniences. Instead of a sink,
they have a board stretched across one corner of a room. When the
washing of the dishes is done, the refuse is thrown out of the back
door. When a woman desires meat for her family, she orders it at the
company store. When the manager receives enough orders of meat, he
kills a cow.

Everything in the village is company owned. The houses
look like barns on stilts, and appear to have been thrown together.
When I would go inside one of them, I could see outside through the
cracks in the walls. The workers do all of their trading at the
company store and bank, and use the company school and library, for
they have no means of leaving the village. The money is kept circu-
lating from the employer to the employees, employees to company store,
store to company bank, and from the bank to the company again. The
result is old torn bills in the pay envelope each week.

I worked in the South for nine months, and during that time I could not reconcile myself to the conditions of the mill and village. Therefore, I left the South and returned to the North - back to the clock punching, speed-up and efficiency system of the northern mills.

Five years have passed since then, and I have learned through experience that I may go North, South, East or West in my search for work, and find miserable working conditions for miserable wages. I know that the workers in any industry are in a most deplorable condition, but the workers of the South are in virtual slavery.

Through the efforts of labor organizations, the workers of the South must be made to understand why they have such conditions. Once they do understand, they, with the backing of labor organizations, will rise up in revolt and demand that which is rightly theirs.

ARTIFICIAL SILK

Artificial silk is made from cotton waste. They make this waste into a liquid form by using different kinds of chemicals, some very strong acids are used. No one knows the secret of making the silk but a few Germans. If the men do not wear the gloves, the acids will eat holes in their hands; if they wear pants with cotton in them, or overalls, they are eaten full of holes in a day or so. The men wear rubber boots or overshoes, because there is water and acids on the floor.

It is dangerous for the men to work in the chemical department. I have known several to lose their eyes by getting something in them. Two, I know of, lost their lives. It is also very unhealthy for the men in the spinning room. Anyone not used to it can hardly get their breath when they first go in, the ammonia is so strong. And the wages are very low for the men.

The textile room is in good sanitary condition. We have plenty of air and plenty of light. But the girls have to work so hard. They work ten hours a day and do not make enough to live on. The girls are all on piece work now. They are supposed to run 65, or 90 pounds (according to the turn) for $1.80 a day, and so much for extra pounds. Some of the girls run as high as 125 pounds a day. About the highest any of them could make would be $14 a week.

After I had been there a year, I was given the job of being a forelady and was paid $16.30 a week. I had to carry passes in my pocket for the girls if they wanted to go to the wash room, and they would have to come and ask me if they could go. Every day they would make new rules and all seemed to be getting harder. If a girl was caught sitting down for one minute, she was discharged; she was not allowed to talk to the girl that worked by her. If I happened to help a girl work and the foreman saw me, I would get something like this: "You are not supposed to help any of these girls, you are to see that they do their work and do it well, and if they can't do it we will send them home."

The girls were not satisfied, but were afraid to say anything. I have heard the girls say it was like a jail, but they had to work somewhere. And the men were being treated in the same way. The men stood it as long as they could, until they had a strike. They did not have a union at that time, and they did not gain anything. Some of them were fired and never allowed to work there again. The company took some of them back, and the ones that went back formed a secret union. The company kept putting more work on them all the time. In January, about half of the girls in our room were laid off, as well as some of the men, for sixty days. The company kept the best operators, of course, and doubled their work, and if one said anything about it they were told that they ought to consider themselves lucky because they still had work. They cut off all the boys that carried bobbins to the girls. The girls had to do that, which took time and meant less wages for them. They did not like it, but all seemed to be afraid to kick about it.

When a nearby mill had the first strike, our girls did not want to strike because they were afraid. Our mill closed down until every thing was settled. An agreement had been made that the union people would be treated as well as the non-union. But our company did not do what they agreed to do. I soon decided to join the union. I talked to several girls and got them to join. I had been a member one week when the next strike happened. The other mill started it. Several hundred came up to our gates. About fifty men and boys climbed the fence and came into the plant. I saw two boys who I knew belonged to the union, and I asked them what they wanted. They told me to strike. I said all right, we will strike. I found five union girls and told them to follow me. We went down stairs and punched our cards, and I went on outside. We were out quite a while and no one followed. I knew there were more union people in there, but they seemed afraid to come out. So we got the boys to open the gate. I never knew how they got it open, but they did and we girls led them back into our mill. We turned off all machines, blew the whistle and ordered out the rest of the workers. Some of them did not want to go out, but they thought it best to do so.

This plant is owned by several different ones. The Germans are the controlling stock holders. There are several company houses. They are nice little four, five, six or eight room houses with water, electricity and a bathroom in most of them. The rent is not as high now as it was before the strike. A small house that was $34 a month is about $22 a month now.

Before the strike, there was no recreation of any kind. The company provides ball games now, and an amusement park, where workers can go on Sunday if they wish. Two big dances have been given since the strike.

A JOB IN A LAUNDRY

I had been out of work for some time before I realized that my leisure had brought disaster upon my already low finances. I had only $5 left, and I had to pay my week's rent. After settling with my landlady, I had $1 left.

I was fortunate, however, in meeting someone who offered me a job in his steam laundry. I accepted gratefully. He told me to report for work the next day. I did not discuss hours or wages, because I was afraid of appearing too bold, and I knew at that moment I could not afford to take any chances.

I began my work on a hot July day. The impressions I got that day will always remain with me. When I came into the place at 8:00, everything was already in full swing. I had never before been in a steam laundry and when I entered that large barn-like place filled with steam, I actually imagined that I had stopped breathing. My first impulse was to turn around and look for the door, but I was too late. The employer had noticed me. He motioned to one of the girls, telling her to show me where the dressing room was, and also to take me over to the shakers. The girl looked at me indifferently, and asked me to follow her. The further we advanced, the more difficult my breathing became. When we came to the farthest end of the place, the air was a little drier, and it was easier to breathe. At last I could see what was going on.

There were about thirty women working on shakers. Each one stood before a table in front of which stood several bags of washed clothes. My arrival aroused no particular interest in the group. The girl told me to observe what the old woman at the table next to mine was doing. After watching for some time, I tried to pick up one of the bags of wet wash, but I found that I could not do it. I felt quite embarrassed when the old woman helped me lift the bag. She assured me, however, that within a day or two I would be able to do it very easily. Lifting the next bag was just as much of a problem as the first had been, but one of the men who brought the work to us, noticing my dilemma, changed my work to smaller bags.

After I had my problem solved, I began taking notice of my fellow workers. Out of the thirty women, ten were between sixteen and twenty years of age; the rest were between forty and sixty. They all looked tired and haggard. The old women were half asleep at their jobs. It was pitiful to see women at an age when they should have been retired, standing in that hell-like heat working.

When I inquired at lunch time of some of the older women the reason for their having to work, each one had a tale of misery to tell. They all agreed, however, that the jobs they had were the best they could get under the circumstances. Laundries were almost the only industry in which they were in demand. In the laundry, they did not have to work very fast. Neither did they have to come in very early, because it takes some time until the work is washed and ready for them.

I did not last very long at my job in the laundry because I refused to work more than eight hours for the $10 that I was getting. The employer would probably have submitted to my conditions because I did twice as much work as the others, but several of the younger workers had asked me why I was so privileged. I told them that if they would refuse to work until 10:00 at night as I did, the employer would have to get used to the idea of parting with them at 6:00. The employer realized that I stirred up the older workers to leave on time, and he told me that work was getting very slow and that he could not keep me any longer.

Having become interested in the conditions of women in that industry, I looked up the statistics of a survey conducted by the Woman's Bureau of the Department of Labor in twenty-three cities in the United States. Out of 24,337 workers, 19,758 were women, one-fourth Negro, three fourths white. Forty-three per cent of the white and 41 per cent of the Negro women were married. White women in the East received for full time the median wage of $17.80 per week, and the colored women $10.25. In the Middle West, the white women received $15.05 and the colored women $13.80; in the South, white, $15.55, Negro, $7.25. The hours women worked in laundries were not any more encouraging than the wages they got. In the East, 80 per cent worked forty-eight hours and under. In the Middle West, 51 per cent worked fifty to fifty-four hours; in the West, 97 per cent, forty-eight hours and under. In the South, 48 per cent worked fifty-four hours and over.

My personal experience and those figures from the survey taken during the prosperity years of 1927-8 have made me realize the vital need for organization in American industry. I hope that in the near future workers will realize that the racial hatred that is being bred by the capitalist class is not to the advantage of the Negro or white worker who should have one common purpose: that of organizing against capitalism.

CANDY WRAPPING

The building in which I work is a large one, five stories high with wooden floors that are kept clean by colored porters who sweep twice daily and mop once a week. The walls are cleaned every year, and some of them are painted. Usually, men who are not needed in slack seasons are given the painting to do, thus keeping them employed full time.

The chocolate room and wholesale department are cooled by the washed air system. There are large double glass windows on all sides of the wholesale department that are never opened. This makes it necessary to burn electric lights, but the lights are well placed so that we are not bothered with poor lighting. The windows in all other parts of the building are well screened and can be opened at any time.

There are two large dressing rooms, with mirrors - one for the boys, and the other for the girls. Each employee has an individual locker for which a key can be had for 35 cents. Each dressing room has two shower baths and a fountain spray.

The drinking water is kept in sanitary coolers, the ice separate from the water. The girls packing on the belt depend for their water on the belt boy, who is kept very busy keeping the belt full of candy. This means the girls do not get water as often as they would like.

There has been only one modern machine introduced in this company since I began working some years ago. Fortunately, no one was displaced by the machine; the girls were given other work in the plant.

The wages are very low, the highest weekly wage of $25 being paid to the forelady. The average is about $12.50 for nine and a half hours daily, with a five and a half day week. In rush seasons, we work overtime, for which straight time is paid. A bonus is paid for a certain amount of candy packed and wrapped - an incentive so that the speediest worker will set a greater pace, and the others are urged to keep up with it.

The work is very tiring, and the rate of speed exhausts the workers. Every day someone will say, "I would like to have gone to a bridge party last night, but I was just too tired"; or, "I could not enjoy the movie last night because I was so tired."

There are no provisions made for old age, and no accident insurance. The workers depend upon the compensation law, but there are few accidents that we have included in this. The only insurance is the group insurance plan. The company pays part of the premium and the employees part, and the insurance carries only death benefits.

The hours are far too long, and the wages too small. The workers must have more time to themselves, and more comforts. The workers want freedom from fear of unemployment, disease and sickness. If workers could only realize that this could be gotten by solidarity, they would get together and organize a union and work toward that purpose.

A SOUTHERN TOBACCO PLANT

The Turkish Plant of one tobacco factory is on the ground floor. It is quite new. It has double fire-proof windows which are fastened by iron bolts and cannot be opened. The window panes are not transparent but do give plenty of light. There are sky-lights also, and in the afternoon the sun shines down on the workers so that it is hard for them to do good work because of the glare.

This plant has a device for warming the building in winter and is supposed to give cool air in the summer. It also has a device for sucking up the tobacco dust and the bronze used in printing; but there is plenty left filtering through the air to go in the lungs of the workers.

There is a sanitary fountain, at which the workers drink water, that is kept cool by a General Electric cooler. The toilets are modern and are built of tile. These are lavatories with hot and cold water. There are also paper towels. This place is kept very clean by a Negro girl, who does nothing else.

This tobacco factory has a medical department of which it is very proud. A doctor and two nurses, one white and one colored, are employed by the company. If a worker is injured while on the job, she is rushed to this hospital, where she may or she may not get immediate medical attention. That depends on whether or not one of the nurses is busy entertaining one of the bosses.

The workers are always clean. The company compels them to wear smocks or uniforms which must be kept clean. The workers are supposed to go to work at 7:30 in the morning; and yet some are forced to be there and to start to work at 7:15. If they are not there they are threatened with the loss of their jobs. When one girl asked if her pay started at 7:15, the boss said, "Hell, no." Then the girl said that she did not think it right that she should start to work before her pay started. "Well," said the boss, "You don't have to, but I can make it so damned hard for you that you will wish you had!"

The workers in this plant work nine hours a day, if there are any orders, with a five minute relief in the morning and one in the afternoon. They have thirty minutes for lunch. There is no cafeteria so they have to eat sitting on skids, containers or anything that is handy. They must eat in the front of the room away from the tobacco or cigarettes. The boss's desk is also up at the front of the room so you can see the situation there. A Negro girl sweeps the floor just as if no one were eating there. This is very disagreeable.

Last summer, machines were installed to pack "flat fifties."

This, of course, put about three hundred girls out of work. Machines that pack "twenties" have been replaced by new ones, and each machine takes work away from three to five girls. The cigarette-making machines have been speeded up in order to keep the packers running. This means that each girl working in the cigarette-making department has to speed up according to the speed of the machine. This is a physical and mental strain. By having to work so fast, they are not able to see all the defects in the cigarettes. The workers' eyes often become affected from the strain. At a time of unemployment, such as the one we now have, there is always the worry of how long they will be able to hold their jobs, even though they pay little.

Many girls become faint and sometimes ill from heat, to-bacco dust, and from the nervous strain of the stretch-out system.

THE PRESIDENT VISITS THE MILL

One day at work, word was received that the President of our tobacco company was coming to visit the plant the next day. The boss sent me around to tell all the workers to get busy and start cleaning their machines. We had a half day to get everything ready for the President.

The next day, when the President came through he had several other men with him, some wearing diamond stick pins and rings which cost thousands of dollars. The President did not look at the cigarettes; he merely looked over the floor. When one of those very important looking men stopped at one of the cigarette machines that was making fourteen hundred cigarettes a minute, he found just one bad cigarette before the girl that was catching could get to it. (It is nothing unusual for a cigarette machine to run a bad cigarette once in a short time.) This man showed the bad cigarette to the President. The President called the foreman and had the girl fired.

This girl had a mother and a little sister to take care of on $11 a week. The men went on their way to another floor, while the girl trudged home with the news that she had no job.

A CIGARETTE FACTORY

I had been in the employ of a cigarette factory for twenty-three months with a very good record. My younger sister who worked beside me was hired the day I was. We had the same foreman and weigher. (The weigher is a girl in charge of six machines who goes to each every half hour, weighs and gauges several handfuls of cigarettes to see that they are running all right.) The weigher was apparently very fond of my sister, for she often told me what a good worker she was.

One Monday morning, my sister's operator did not come in. Without an operator, it is difficult to keep the cigarettes running well, for he has quite a lot to do with paste, tobacco, paper, bronze, print and size. Her cigarettes began to pop open. She asked the mechanic to run her machine until the foreman could send her an operator. He refused, and forbade her stopping it.

When the foreman came along and found bad work on her machine he told her that if she passed any more bad work he would have to fire her. She stopped the machine when her work began to run bad again, and began picking out the imperfect cigarettes. While the machine was stopped, the section and general foreman came along and fired her. That made me mad for I knew they had no right to fire her under the circumstances. When the vice-president came along presently, I asked him if there was any chance of my sister getting her job back. He told me he would do all he could for her.

The foreman saw me talking to him and guessed what was up, so he came on over to my machine and asked me just what I was talking to Mr. A. about. When I told him, he said "I would like to see you at the desk." I followed him and was not long in learning that if I wished to keep my job I would have to keep quiet. He said, "I fired her, and as long as I work here she will never work here again." (He was in charge of hiring employees at that time.) I went back to work for the rest of the day, but I saw that they wanted to get rid of me before I caused trouble. All the bad work which was found on the packers was brought to my machine and I was accused of it. Knowing that I would not stay a week longer without being fired for someone else's work, I did not go back after that day.

A friend of our family is a close friend of the superintendent. He told him how my sister had been treated. On Saturday night that week, they both came to our home and asked sister to tell them all about getting fired. When she had finished, Mr. G. asked for a piece of paper and wrote, "Please re-employ B.G." and signed his name. He told her to go back to work on Monday. When she gave this note to the man who fired her, he read it and looked at her for a minute as if he did not know what it was all about. Then he asked where she got it. His next question was "Where is your sister?" She told him I had another job. He re-employed her and sent her back to the same foreman.

BEAN PICKING

About the middle of June every year, Mother would take us four children out to some country place to work. We usually picked beans. This was a back-breaking job. We had to be up at 4:30 every morning, go in the fields at 5:30, and work until dusk. If the crops were good, we made on an average of $15 to $17 a day. Some of the large families made as much as $25 to $30 a day. We were paid a penny a pound.

The shacks in which we lived were shabby, run-down, one room affairs. We had no electric bills. The wood was supplied by the boss. We usually ate what we could take from the fields. Therefore, we had very little expense.

The beds were made of straw piled on the floor and covered with sheets. The whole family slept in one bed. Whenever it rained, we would have to have pots under the places where the roof leaked. We had to make our own stoves from bricks and mud paste. Sometimes the stove would fall apart when it rained and we would have to make another one.

At night we would gather around the fire, from where we could see the bossman's home. A big, beautiful white home on the hill, surrounded by shrubbery, trees and flowers. We were not allowed to walk on his property - he said we would ruin his flowers.

Sometimes while working in the fields, some of the young boys and girls would start singing. The boss man would come over and tell us to stop. He said it made him nervous and, besides, we should work and not sing.

His son came home from college about this time. He would talk to us and be friendly while his father was not around, but he never recognized any of us when we went to town and he was among his own class.

One day the boss came to our shacks and insisted on searching them. We did not know what it was all about, but we soon found out. Some of his chickens were missing and he accused us of stealing them. The people could stand being accused of almost anything but stealing. We called a strike and refused to go to work the next morning. The boss tried to force us, but he saw it was no use. The next day he hired a truck and sent us home.

WHY I OPPOSE NIGHT WORK

I worked five months on the night shift. My work began at 6:00 in the afternoon, and stopped at 5:00 in the morning. The mill was hot, since there had been no fresh air in it all day. It was most unbearable when we began our work at night. In summer time, the heat was worse. The windows were raised about two feet from the bottom, with blank windows at the top. "Any more air would prevent the work from running all right," so the bossman said.

When I first began night work, I had a good appetite and ate my supper regardless of the heat. But after a month's time, I did not want anything. We had to eat in the mill, just anywhere we could find a clean spot. Most of us ate in the spool room on a turned-up roping box, while the lint in the air went into our food. If we did not have time to leave our work to go to the spool room, we ate on the floor beside our frame where there was more cotton and lint in the air than in the spool room, besides the oil and tobacco spit on the floor. We were not given any time off for supper. Most of the time, if I did want to eat, I had no time to stop. The work usually ran badly. The ends came down so fast that in ten minutes the sides would have been in a mess. In the first four hours, I slept very well; but after the people began their daily work I would wake up and could not get any more sleep that day. In the evening, when I went to work, I could not tell I had had those few hours' rest.

All the workers, both men and women, felt the way I did — completely exhausted and old before their time. I think the law should not only prohibit night work for women, but for men also. No men or women can stand the strain of night work under such conditions.

AN ILL WIND

One loud shriek — then screams.

"Turn off the power!"

"Get a doctor!"

"Bring some water!"

More shrieking and screaming.

Girls fell to the floor like flies. Some girls were sick to their stomachs. Other people ran back and forth.

Then one girl came running down the aisle with her hand up to her head. It looked as if she were wearing a white skull cap. Blood streamed down her back. She ran into the dressing room. This girl had been scalped.

The bobbin fell from the machine; she reached underneath to pick it up, and her hair was caught in the bolt. This all happened in a few minutes, but it seemed like hours to the ones who witnessed the sight. The girl was rushed to the hospital in the machine of one of the workers. During all the time the girl was conscious until they arrived at the hospital.

The accident happened about 11:00 on a Thursday morning. The shop had to be completely closed down for the day, for no one could resume her work.

This girl was in the hospital for some time; then the state compensation was to be granted. As in all cases, it was thoroughly investigated. It was found the young woman was pregnant at the time of the accident, and no allowance could be given. There is a law in our state that no woman under these conditions can work in a factory. Just how this was settled I do not know, but at one time I heard the company was giving her some kind of allowance.

But this much I can say: the workers received some good from this terrible accident. The very next day screens were placed in front of every machine in the place. The manager passed this remark to me, a few days later, "When the horse is stolen, we lock the stable."

It is an ill wind that blows nobody good.

THE MANIT SYSTEM

In the year 1931, the Manit system was installed in our mill. This system was one of task setting and efficiency rating to determine how much can be done by a worker engaged in a given operation within a given time.

In using this system in our department, two factors have to be considered: the size of a box and grade of paper used. The rating is very complicated, and we workers never know how much we make at the end of a day's work. Most of the workers resent this very much, and consider the Manit system merely as a speeding up method and a sweat system.

I think this system was supposed to safeguard against over-fatigue and over-exhaustion. But this is not true in our mill. After working for eight hours and handling hot corrugated boxes, most girls are too tired to walk home. I know that they have to use liniment to massage their arms so that their arms will not ache the next day. Therefore, I know that the element of fatigue is not considered in our factory.

The Manit system is supposed to weaken the solidarity of shop groups and stress the competitive power of the individual worker. On the contrary, it has strengthened the solidarity of the workers in our shop. We have organized a union to show our employer we know what tactic he is using in increasing competition.

Also, it is supposed to make the relatively unskilled more efficient and able to receive greater earnings. This is untrue in our shop. The management has used unscrupulous tactics in increasing the output rate, if the individual puts out more than the set rate. The worker, then, becomes suspicious and never tries to work harder than is absolutely necessary. For instance, if the set rate is to fold 1000 boxes an hour for 35 cents, and the girls fold 1200 boxes within an hour, their wages increase automatically to 42 cents an hour. But the management sees this, and increases the output rate to 1200 an hour for 35 cents. Or, if the set rate is higher than the worker can make, we make out our report according to the rate set, instead of the actual number of boxes folded.

Time and motion study is to insure pay according to efficiency, to secure justice for each worker. Again, I would like to point out that this is not true. Time and motion study has taught the worker to be suspicious of his employer, and has also taught the worker to try to cheat the company whenever possible.

THE PIECE-WORK SYSTEM

I suggest that those people who invented piece-work be given
a chance to work on that basis, under the same conditions as we piece-
workers do, and see how they would like it.

I think that piece-work is a very unjust method of paying
workers. If we realized how piece-work harms us mentally and physi-
cally, we might take it a little bit more seriously. Piece-work is
paid on a plan that is more like guess-work than anything else. The
employer cannot resist the temptation to cut prices when he sees that
we are making more than he thinks we ought to make.

Often the employer picks the fastest girl in the place and
gives her a certain amount of work to turn out, with a time-study
method of ascertaining the time required. When she turns out more
than the average worker, and so earns more, the employer usually cuts
the prices accordingly. He may cut the rate again and again. And we
have to work faster and faster in order to get a living wage. Our
work is seasonal, so we are forced to make as much as we can to save
some money for the slack time. The result is, that we get tired, disagreeable, and sometimes sick, so that we have to stay at home for a
few days in the full season. I know a great number of girls who have
been working long years in industry under the speed-up system who
have heart disease or some other serious sickness.

Must we always be needlessly sacrificed to the desire for
profit of the employers? Can not we discover some sort of "scien-
tific management" which has as its aim the protection of the health
and happiness of the workers, instead of the piling up of profits
for the employers?

THE EFFECT OF EMPLOYMENT ON ONE'S HEALTH

The great cry of today is, "I am unemployed." This is one instance I would like to give to show where unemployment might have been better for me.

I worked in a radio factory. I had a job called scraping. The process was to take a small "coil," a coil which had two copper ends or wires to it. These ends were put on a stool blade protruding from a wooden block, and scraped. This process was as easy as it sounds. It was only easy to do. But there was something about it that got on everyone's nerves. I was the first girl to do the operation in this way. Until this time, the work had been done an entirely different way, making this an altogether new process.

Everything was fine and dandy for a while. I got along all right, until I began to find when I left the shop at nights I was awfully nervous. I would get into arguments with the girls at work over nothing at all. One day, while I was working, very peacefully, indeed, I suddenly began to feel very shaky. I felt as though I were going to scream. I laid down my razor blade and put my hands to my head and to my amazement I was seized with a violent trembling and I seemed to be screaming at the top of my voice. After that things seemed rather vague. I remember feeling cold water dashed in my face. Some one asked, " Did she cut her finger?" Others wanted to know if I were sick. Then I found myself in the dispensary. I had been carried there by some of the men that worked near me. I lay there very quiet for a while, trying to figure out just what had happened to me. I felt shaky and nervous. I tried to sleep, but it was useless. The nurse had given me some medicine and I felt after a while as though I would be able to go back to my work.

Before I started working, I asked my foreman if I could go home. We were very busy at the time and he said he could not spare me. I went back to my place and tried to work. It was no use; I could not do it. My hand trembled so I could not hold the blade. I just put my head down and cried. I did not know why I was crying; I just could not help it. When the foreman saw this, he told me to go home; he would get some one to take my place.

I went home and rested that day and the next morning I went back to work. The foreman acted rather distant and cold. I expected him to lay me off before I even started to work. I found out later that they had had a hard time finding some one who was fast enough to take my place, so they had to have two girls do the job.

I was all right for about a week. Then out of a clear sky the same thing happened, and three days later it happened again. By that time I was frightened and went to a doctor. He told me it was overwrought nerves. He also said that I should change my job. When I told

the foreman this he changed me for one day. But the next morning
found me right back on the old job again. I stayed on it until the
rush season was over, about two months later. I had two more spells
similar to the previous ones, only not quite as violent. Each time
I was put back to my job and not sent home.

When the rush season was over I was laid off. I was told
they could not keep me on as I was always sick. Since I left there
the spells have not been as frequent but I still have recurrences
of them at times, although before I was put on that operation I had
never known what it was to be nervous.

OPEN SHOPS AND COMPANY UNIONS

SPYING IN A SWEAT SHOP

My one day experience working in a company union dominated
sweat shop is the most thrilling of my life.

During the month of August I was called to this city to organize for a union in the clothing industry. In order to learn the
conditions under which an employee must work in a company union dominated shop, I felt that it would be essential for me to be employed
there for a limited time. Donning a disguise, I journeyed to this shop
and asked for a job. After relating my experience as a hemmer, I was
ushered to the third floor, to be interviewed by the manager. I finally convinced him I was O. K., and reported for work as a hemmer the
following day. And what a day!

During the course of the morning I became thirsty and retired to the rest room. To my amazement the spigot of the ice cooler was
broken. A filthy rag was jammed into the spigot, forcing the workers
to adopt the unsanitary method of dipping their drinking cups. As the
day wore on, the heat became terrific. The windows being painted dis-
play windows, it was utterly impossible to open them. You can imagine
our discomfort – we who were thirsty, and hot! I could scarcely
breathe, and oh! what a relief at noon hour when I went outside for
some air. In front of the shop were some strikers from another shop,
which is now a union shop, passing out literature.

After the noon hour, workers were whispering here and there
about a company union meeting at 3:30 P.M. which was to be held on the
floor. I was very anxious to attend this meeting. Before the meeting
the forelady informed four of the workers, who were members of the
clothing union, that they could not attend. She said, "I am the proud
possessor of a petition signed by twenty-six workers (certainly not the
majority) asking the dismissal of the four trouble makers," who they
assumed were members of the outside union, as they called our trade
union. These four workers were not allowed to come to the meeting to
defend themselves.

At the meeting, the forelady, also the chair-lady, called
upon the vice president, who was the "cutter boss" and highly compen-
sated by the firm for the job he was doing for the company union. He
spoke very highly of the good union they had, saying: "The boss is
cooperating with us 100 per cent; you can already see he has helped
us dismiss these four trouble makers. We may see a picket line in
the morning in front of the shop, but don't be afraid. I am your
'captain' and your machines are your artillery. Call me by phone
and I will protect you." I could not imagine this stool-pigeon pro-
tecting any person, as already he was shaking like a leaf in a storm.
Nevertheless the workers applauded, not realizing that some day they
too would be dismissed in the same illegitimate manner as were the
above four workers.

By then my heart was bleeding when I realized how those workers were traitors to their fellow workers. The meeting was opened for grievances. Characteristic of a company union, no grievances were submitted. After a lengthy period, however, a worker yelled: "Yes, I have a grievance. We have a spy in our factory. Where is she? Bring her to the front." I was singled out. The vice president insisted on pulling me to the front. I was asked if I was a member of the workers' union, and I replied, "Yes, and I am proud of the fact. No, I am no spy, but just an American citizen surprised at the conditions you are willing to tolerate. Straighten your jelly-fish backs and throw your chests out. Become members of our union, an organization which gives you the right to bargain collectively so you no longer will have to see your fellow workers dismissed for no good reason as you have today. Your company union is not the law of the land; therefore, it is not true Americanism to belong to a company union. You do not get a decent wage, you do not even have what God rightfully provides you with, and that is fresh air and pure water."

Strange as it may seem I was allowed to go on with my speech until, at this point, someone screamed, "Wipe up the floor with her." I did not fear this statement, for any person who does not have the courage to assert his rights as a worker will not have the courage to wipe the floor with a labor union member. After much commotion and controversy, I was booed by a woman who, I assumed, was forced to work in the shop due to economic conditions. I asked the woman if she was a mother of children and she replied very proudly "Yes, I have a daughter and a son." I said, "I am also a mother of children, but I am fighting to make a better and more decent place to live in, and some day you'll rue the day you booed just another mother." The booing ceased and I was accompanied to the office by the company union president, who was afraid to leave me alone, as I may have told the "captain's army" the truth.

When I arrived in the office to receive my pay, which was $1.20 for eight hours work as an experienced operator, I found the four heroes who were dismissed by their fellow workers demanding an explanation for the injustice given them. The boss's only reply was, "the company union members fired you." The girls told the boss he know a company union was not the law of the land. He replied he was aware of this fact, but as long as he could get away with it he was going to take a chance.

The four heroes went to the company union grievance committee, but that committee talked about mops for the floor. We marched out of the shop singing our union songs, challenging ourselves to fight this sweat shop to the finish.

This true story should teach anyone that a company union is nothing but an exercise of influence over workers by the boss.

THE "ONE BIG FAMILY" SHOP

The largest clothing factory in Ohio is the R---- Brothers'
Shop. They had no children of their own so they adopted their employees. Miss Anna when very young had been a household employee in
the home of the parents of the R---- brothers. The oldest boy had
her educated so she could work in the office. And now she is a boss.
Once during the first five years I worked in the old department, the
manager had a disagreement with Miss Anna. So he had to go. The
Superintendent also had a disagreement with Miss Anna, and he had to
go. Miss Anna is strongly built, plain looking and plainly dressed,
a woman without a heart or soul! Cold penetrating eyes! But she
could be very sweet when she needed a girl. After two years of working there, I sprained my wrist very badly. I had an x-ray taken, and
stayed home a little over two weeks. It was two days before Chris-
mas - we all got two weeks vacation with pay, free chicken dinner,
and dancing after dinner. We have dancing at lunch hour every day.
I used to think this was wonderful.

When they opened in January, I had to report to the doctor.
My wrist was still swollen. The doctor talked to Miss Anna and then
she talked to me in a very sweet way, "Will you try and sew, and if
you can't stand the pain you come down, dear, and we will see what we
can do for you." I came down. I had a leather strap around my wrist.
The doctor took this one off and put an elastic one on and sent me
back to work again. They needed me very badly as one of the girls,
who had done the same work, was sick with rheumatism. So I worked
with a terrible pain. I thought I would lose my arm. But I had my
two weeks of Christmas pay and in July we used to get one week's
vacation with pay again. And this must be appreciated, I thought.
Big fool that I was. Before holidays we always had a free chicken
dinner. After dinner the Senior Partner spoke to us, and said he
wanted us to appreciate this. Even though there was no other firm
in our city giving Christmas vacation pay, R---- Brothers would continue to do so. As he had no children of his own he had adopted us
all as his children. So this is how we had become the biggest
Family in Ohio. We were told to buy stock - in fact we had to buy
it - and were told not to sell it. The Family should share the
profit with the company.

Any one working there was considered lucky. Reporters
came there and asked the girls, "How do you like to work here?"
"Oh just fine." And then they put big articles in the paper.
What a wonderful place this was to work in! No bosses, no clock.
No bosses! I never saw so many of them in any place. In every department they had a manager, a head foreman, an assistant foreman,
and for every table one, two, or three examiners. There were sixteen machines to every table. If one examiner did not find fault
with the work another one did, or the head foreman would find some-

thing wrong with it.

The head foreman was called Frank, "the monkey." He resembled more an ape than a human being. The Bohemian girls gave him this name. One Saturday morning I had no work. It was almost 10:00 o'clock. I went up to "the monkey" and asked for a pass to go home, and told him that the Bohemian girl was working on two bundles. "And if I can't get work here I've got work to do at home." So he yelled out at me, "I don't give a damn if you've got work or not. You stayed out last week two days when I needed you. Now you stay in too." "But I was sick last week." "I don't care. You stay in."

Then on another occasion the collars were cut one inch too short. I could not get them worked in as the collar would be stretched, and the coat lining would show folds. I was fooling around with this all morning. So I showed it to the foreman. "The collars are too short. I can't sew them in." He called Monkey. Well he sewed one in. It took him over half an hour. And how did the coat look? We were getting 2 cents for one collar. So he said, "See I got it in." Said I, "You can't expect me to take two days to work on twenty coats. I am on piece work." "I don't give a damn if it takes you two weeks. You get me? If I can get it in you can too." Tears were rushing to my eyes. I was trembling all over. I thought of my child. I must work, I can not lose self-control. Working here I can go home for lunch as I live close by, and have lunch with my child. The next thing I knew I was in the sick room. I heard somebody say, "Did she sew her finger?" I looked at my fingers. There was nothing wrong. Then I realized what had happened. I heard in the next room Miss Anna say, "Oh, she is so tender hearted she can't stand a calling down."

Katherine, the girl next to me, went on Monday to ask Miss Anna whether she could have her pay from last week. Her sister was going to a convent and she wanted to buy her the necessary things. Miss Anna said, "Can't you save your money like the rest of the girls. Every week you come here and want your pay in advance." "Why Miss Anna this is the second time in four years." Miss Anna: "I know better." The Senior Partner was in the office and Miss Anna made him believe that "some people need a good bawling out."

Katherine came up crying, "Never again will I ask her for my money." "Yes," said I, "if this was a union shop we could do something about it." Next week I was sent down to the office.

Miss Anna greeted me with, "What do I hear about you?" "I don't know what you mean Miss Anna."

"Did you say anything about a strike?"

"Do I look crazy?"

"Well, we don't want anybody to work here, if he is not satisfied. You can have your pay right now."

"You know Miss Anna I have to work."

I was given another chance. They opened a new department.
I was transferred. My work too was changed. I had to sew in sleeves,
and got 55 cents an hour. I had been making 80 cents an hour. This
was hell again. John, the foreman, was a Bohemian about four feet
ten, and weighed 115 pounds. Once on a Monday morning John came in
in a terrible humour, picked up my work and gave it back to me and
said, "If you wouldn't get drunk on Sunday you could do your work
right on Monday." He repeated this about three times. I cried out
and told him, "I won't stand for it. I never was drunk in my life."
Then he told me, "The boss asks every day 'how is Agnes doing her
work?' I tell: 'no good, no good, and have you fired.'" One of the
girls went up to the boss and asked him, "Why don't you do something
about John? It is terrible the way the girls get insulted in your
department." Well John got transferred to a different department.

For about eight months things went well. We had Holland
Pete, and it was heaven. Then he was changed to a higher position.
Another devil came. The last two months I cried every day. I never
saw so many girls cry in my seventeen years of factory experience.
At last I broke down. I was five weeks sick at home. When I reported to work again I was told by Miss Anna that my job was taken. I
said to her, "But you know, Miss Anna, that I can do all the operations in this place, and you are hiring over thirty girls today."

"I sent for those girls so I must give them work. I'll
send for you in a week. There'll be something in your line."

I knew she never would. And here I was one of the children.
I belonged to the big Family, and was a stock holder of the company
too. I thought I had a life job.

I CAN CHANGE MY NAME, BUT NOT MY FACE

I had been out of work for a long time; it was impossible to get a job. Finally, I saw an advertisement in the paper: "Experienced operators on dresses wanted, P----- Dress Company."

Though I tried to be the first one, I found a few girls already waiting for the employer. Some more came in. We exchanged words until 8:30.

Then, out from the office came a tall, strong, red-headed, unfriendly looking man, who asked each girl separately on what and where she had worked before, and then sent her to the dressing room. I was the last one.

"Well," he said to me, "what kind of work did you do?"

"I am experienced on silk and cotton dresses," I said. I named a few factories in which I had worked.

"Oh, well," he answered, "but you can't work here."

"Why can't I? I am experienced. I make a fine garment. Give me the opportunity to prove it. Four workers know me. Ask them."

"I don't take advice from any employee when I need help, and you will not get any work here," he said in a high voice.

"Oh, I wanted so much to work today. The money is all gone, and the rent was due last week. I must have a job."

I decided to speak to the girls. Maybe they can do something for me. I saw them coming. Some I knew; some I did not know. It did not matter; I would have spoken to them anyway.

"Listen, girls, you know how long I have been out of work. Your boss needs operators, and he will not take me. It is up to you to see that I get work here. Go over in a large group to him and tell him that you want me to work here, or you will not work. The factory is busy, and he will not want any trouble; you can have your way."

The girls hesitated. It was an unorganized shop. They were afraid they would lose their jobs. "All right," replied a dark eyed, thin girl, "we will try our utmost. Either we are fired, or you'll be with us." It took a few minutes. She rushed out from the elevator. "Come up, but be careful. He has your number. Try to make your work better than usual. We had a fight. Oh, what a fight we had. I will tell you later."

No matter how carefully I made the work, I got it back to

fix. Every time someone else would find fault with it. Whenever my machine got spoiled, I had to wait a long time before the machinist would fix it. Then, of course, I got the work which was not so well paid. This place discouraged me. What was the matter that I could not make a cheap dress? I had always worked on a good line. I began to lose self-confidence, and became worried. I know I was almost done with this city if I lost that job. During the two years that I had spent there, I had been fired from many shops for organization activity. But I did not do much here.

As I was thinking, the forelady burst out to me: "Listen, sixty-six!" (That was my number. In a big factory, you lose your name. A number is enough for a worker.)

"What is it?" I answered.

"What do you mean by talking all day long to the girls? That is the reason why your work is rotten."

"Let me see what is wrong, and I will fix it."

"Oh never mind fixing. We can't use your work. You should be ashamed of yourself, keeping up friendship with these Negroes. You should stick to your race."

Her speech annoyed me, and I wondered why she spent so much time with me. I realized that I was being watched, and that I would not exist there long.

The Negro pressers got a wage cut, and I talked to them. I told them not to accept the cut, and they listened to me. They were called into the office, and I heard Mr. K. screaming that the girls had the best conditions in town; they even had a radio to listen to. He told them not to listen to silly talk of crazy heads; that he was like a father to them, providing them with work they should appreciate. They should be faithful to him and never complain, since he tried to do his best for them. The pressers listened to the argument, but did not agree to the reduction. At 6:00 that evening, they had not yet settled.

I came in the next day. Everything looked all right, and everybody was working. But when I asked for work, Mr. K. himself came over and said with a sarcastic smile, "There is no work for you, Madame Organizer."

"There is work in the shop," I said.

"There you are," he said. "You see too much and you are too smart!"

"Must I be exactly dumb to know how to make dresses?"

"Sixty-six," he said, "let your union pay you wages. You are a trouble maker in a shop. Why were you fired in B., W., and L. - and in all the other shops? I fire you - take your hat and coat and go."

I could not do much but leave. It was an open shop. The workers were not ready for a stoppage, and the dull season was coming. If some were to rise up, they might lose their jobs. I had better leave this place quietly. I went into the dressing room to get my smock. M., who had watched me all the time, asked, "Why are you fired?"

"Oh, he has my record. I don't know how. He even named the factories where I worked."

"Why don't you change your name?"

Yes, I could change my name, but I could not change my face.

THE EIGHT-CENT DRESS

It all happened when I left P.'s. I did not want to make dresses and suits at 25 cents, so I left. I met T. who worked in J.'s and she told me he needed operators. I climbed up three flights of stairs and walked into the office. What a funny office. A cardboard partition separated the office from the work-room. The shop was very small. There was a long cutting table which extended from one end of the room to the other. There were sixteen machines. In one corner of the room was the finishing table and the racks for the pressed dresses. In the other corner were three pressing machines. Just picture all these things in a room no larger than a three-room apartment. I asked J. if he needed any operators. He asked me where I had worked and what line of dresses I made. I told him and he seemed satisfied. I did not ask him the price he was paying for operating, as one of the girls told me. He told me to come in the next morning. I went in the next morning and he gave me a bundle of five suits. I sat down and started to work. It took me all morning to make them, and I made 65 cents a half day.

When I went home, he told T. "What kind of an operator did you bring me? I want production." It was quite hard for me to work on this cheap line as I had been working on a better line, where they were very fussy with the work. All they wanted here was production. Just so the dresses were put together, that is all that mattered to them. After several days, I got used to them. I worked several weeks and the season ended. A few good workers (not producers) were left to make the samples, and the new season had begun. We were going to make dresses for $1 a dozen. The girls fussed and fumed, but after much arguing, decided to make them. What was the use of arguing, this was better than nothing.

One day we had quite a rumpus. There was not much work and some of the girls had more work than others. The girls who did not have the work complained. The boss calmed us down, and said from now on the work would be divided. What a long wait we had. Well, what could be done? This was better than nothing.

At last the climax came. He cut a new style which looked quite hard to make. I asked one of the girls, "Are we going to make this dress for 8 cents?" Well, she answered, "I think it's all right." In every shop there is always someone who disagrees. Several of us took bundles and started to work on them. The sleeve had three rows of shirring on the top, one row on the bottom, and a lining had to be sewed in. The front and back skirts had three pieces which had to be sewed together. This had to be hemmed and sewed on. Bias had to be pieced, sewed, trimmed and stitched double evenly. The dress was then put together, the bottom hemmed and the dress was finished - all for 8 cents. This was too much for me, so

I told the girls I would not make it. I stopped working. Several
of the girls got up, but some were still working. We put our coats
on and told J. we were through as we did not want to make that dress
for that price. We wanted more money. He called the manufacturer
and a few minutes later the manufacturer walked into the shop, well-
dressed, looking like a million dollars. He seemed so unconcerned
in talking to us. After much discussion, we got a 3 cent raise, so
we all went back to work. The next week we worked on a different
dress for which we got 8 cents. The week after that, the same dress
we got 11 cents for was back at 8 cents again. The girls made it
just the same without complaining. A few weeks later the boss gave
us a raise, which surprised us very much. Imagine giving us a raise
without being asked for it. But he had a purpose, as the next week
the strike broke out.

DISCHARGED

The rumor of a 10 per cent wage cut spread in the shop like
a fire. You could hear of nothing else, but "wage cut," and "10 per
cent." There were differences of opinion about it. Some of the girls
would say that a wage cut is better than a lay off. Others sympathized
with the boss, and defended him loyally. Only a few thought that it
was not fair to cut our wages again, but they were afraid of their jobs,
so they kept quiet. I was at a loss, but not knowing what to do myself,
I went up to the union office, and reported the whole situation. A
leaflet was issued, pointing out the planned attack of the bosses to cut
our wages as much as they could, and encouraging the workers to resist
the wage cut. I talked to the girls, pointing out to them the necessity
of being united and showing the bosses that they can not go on doing
whatever they want to. A few were convinced, but the majority dis-
agreed with me. "Why can't you mind your own business?" they would
ask. "Can't we handle our own affairs?" I felt terribly discouraged.
"Will they ever realize that they can't handle their affairs in such a
manner?" Finally the boss came up, and delivered a pathetic speech.
He was actually in tears when he told us how sorry he was to cut our
wages. He tried to convince us that we would rather have a wage cut
than a lay off. And not waiting for any reply, he left.

Conditions in the place became unbearable. The forelady
would not let us alone. Lectures about making the work better followed, different kinds of complaints and they went so far as to fine
a girl 25 cents for a repair. If you happen to have three repairs
in one week you would be discharged. The shop turned into hell on
earth. Every minute a different girl would pale, when she was called
to the examining table. I kept on talking to the girls, showing them
the audacity of the boss, who not being satisfied with the wage cut,
made us do better work, and threatened to fire us.

A few days elapsed, and with each day a certain hostility
from a few girls grew towards me. Occasionally I would hear some of
them fling the word, "bolsheviki." I knew well enough whom it was
meant for, but I feigned ignorance. I was being watched and annoyed.
The forelady would come around every once in a while and examine my
work, and, not finding any fault with it, would try to antagonize me
in every possible way. "Well, D.," she would say, "I heard that
you're not satisfied with the prices here. Why don't you look for
another job?" The blood mounted to my face. "Well," I answered,
"as soon as I'll get a job, I'll let you know about it." I was left
alone, for the rest of the day. At 5:30 P.M. another leaflet was
passed around, calling the dress and shirt makers to a mass meeting.
I waited for the other girls to come down, and I persuaded them to
come to the meeting. They promised me to come, but they did not show
up at the meeting. A Negro presser was there from our place, and the
organizer introduced me to her. (I did not know her, because the

pressers are working on a different floor.) She told me the same story.
The girls would not come; they were afraid of their jobs. We were very
much interested in the procedure of the meeting, and did not notice that
one of the boss's pets was watching us. I found it out soon enough
though.

The next morning, I was told that there was no more work for
me. The forelady was coaxing me to make it snappy. Although I could
expect to be discharged, still it was such a shock to me, that I did
not know what was going on around me. When I found myself on the
street with my pay envelope in my hand, I realized fully what happened.
I reproached myself bitterly. "Why didn't I raise hell at least? Why
didn't I explain to the girls why I was fired? Why didn't I tell them
all I wanted to say about things that mounted to my head? What a darn
fool I was?"

AN EXPERIENCE WITH A SWEATSHOP BOSS

In 1924 I moved to a large eastern industrial city, from a small country town in the southwestern part of Florida. I found the living conditions somewhat different from what I had been accustomed to, and saw it was necessary for me to go to work to help balance the family budget. As I lived in the mill district I found work in a near-by hosiery mill. A neighbor who was the forelady of the mill took me in and taught me topping.

While learning I thought it was the hardest thing I had ever tried to do, but after a month or two I was getting along fine and only needed to acquire speed. In most of the hosiery work speed is a very important thing as you must be able to keep up with a machine.

After about a month, when they saw I was going to stick, I was asked to join the union, which I did. I was very fortunate in having steady work, good pay, and nice working conditions until the depression came along. After I had worked steady for seven years, the firm I was then working for, packed up and in December, 1932, moved out of the city. I found myself one of the unemployed.

I tried to find work, tramping the streets day after day, in and out of mills, always hearing the same thing, "nothing today." I tried answering some of the advertisements in the Help Wanted columns. Out of about thirty, I received one reply. This was from a sweatshop boss, but when I answered the advertisement, I did not know that.

This answer asked me to come to a certain mill at 1:30 that day. When I arrived I was told to wait as the boss was out to lunch. After waiting for about an hour, I asked the office girl when she expected him back and she said, "any minute now," and asked if I could wait a little longer. Finally the phone rang, and after talking for about five minutes she came and told me the boss was detained. Would I mind coming back tomorrow? Yes, I would mind coming back tomorrow, but I said I could come back even though I knew I must walk home so I would have car fare for the next day. It was only three miles home and walking is good exercise anyway.

The next morning found me waiting again. When the boss arrived, I was called in the office. In a loud roaring voice, he asked me where I had worked last, why I left, how much I made, if I was living with my people, how many were in the family, how many were working, how much they made, and a dozen other questions. He had me so frightened I hardly knew what I was saying. He said since I was living at home and my father working part time, he would not be able to pay me such a large salary, but I seemed like

a nice girl and he would do me a favor and find me a job. I asked
him what would it be, and he said, "Oh! just doing odd jobs around
the shop. It won't be hard." The pay would be $4 per week. The
hours from 2 P.M. till 11 P.M. The first two weeks I would receive
no pay, but after that I could have steady pay as long as I cared
to work.

I was so shocked at the offer that I could not speak for
a few minutes, but when I found my tongue I told him to take his
job and go to the devil, that I refused to work for such starvation
wages. This made him blue in the face with anger and he started
yelling that such ungrateful people as I should starve. I made a
hasty exit, leaving him cursing and swearing.

MY EXPERIENCE IN A COMPANY UNION MILL

The ------ Hosiery Mill situated in the Middle West is one
of the largest in the United States. It employes over three thousand
workers. I started working there June, 1929. I signed the Yellow
Dog Contract not knowing what it was. This read, "I am employed by,
and work for, ------ Hosiery Mills, Inc. and will not affiliate with
any outside organization while employed, nor advise any other employee to do so."

After working several weeks the departmental director came
to me and asked me to join the E.M.B.A., the company union. She told
me of the benefits, such as group insurance, medical attention, sick
benefits, social activities, and protection of the employees against
unfair discharge. Membership was 60 cents a month, which was deducted
from my check. I joined, understanding it was supposed to be a protection to me. I filled in an application, and was given a small card
signifying I was an E.M.B.A. member.

During the first year, I saw girls discharged in a way that
seemed unjust and I could not understand why. Upon asking girls why
this was, they usually answered "inefficiency" or "not the right kind
of spirit." The only reason I could see was that the forelady or foreman did not like these girls. If the girls went to the departmental
director, who was supposed to take up all grievances to the E.M.B.A.
their troubles were seldom adjusted. She, too, was afraid that if
she did take these disputes to the E.M.B.A. she would lose her job.
The question in my mind was, what could be done? I soon learned
there was no remedy at the time.

In November, it seemed as if the boss was trying to keep
something from us. Even girls were secretive. Several weeks later
I learned what had happened. Organizers for a hosiery union had
been trying to organize the knitters into the union but were un-
successful. The company succeeded in getting an injunction against
the organizers and some of the workers for these activities. The
knitters were discharged for violating the Yellow Dog Contract. I
began to see why things had been so quiet, and realized, too, that
the E.M.B.A. and the Yellow Dog Contract were not a protection to
us. Conditions remained the same until the adoption of the N.R.A.
code which said the workers had the right to collective bargaining.

At the request of some of the knitters, union organizers
again came to our city. We were afraid we would lose our jobs if
we joined this union. Some of the knitters had been discharged.
We held secret meetings with other girls to discuss these problems
and often met at drug stores, the Y.W.C.A. and lunch rooms. In
this way we did get a number of girls interested.

The knitters were organizing rapidly now, even though some

were discharged for activities. The company claimed they were discharged for inefficiency; the organizers claimed they were discharged
for their union activities. The cases were taken to the Regional
Labor Board for hearings. The Board ruled that the knitters should
be reinstated and paid lost wages as the company failed to show that
those men had been discharged for inefficiency. They were reinstated.

During our organizing the management was holding meetings
within the different departments, telling the employees it would be
best to stick with the E.M.B.A. because it was the only thing that
had ever helped us, and anyway we were all "one big happy family."

The union had grown so rapidly that a vote was called to
decide which union should represent the employees, the labor union
or the E.M.B.A. While voting, we employees were herded through a
passage under the mill, and given a speech before leaving the building. We were advised to vote for the E.M.B.A., if we considered our
jobs. The election was held across the street from the main entrance
of the mill, and we were not allowed to talk to anyone. Every employee in the mill voted, and the vote was in favor of the E.M.B.A. -
2,016 to 1,054. The vote was protested by our organizers, who claimed only 1,700 were eligible to belong to the labor union. Nothing
was done, however, but we continued building up our union during the
winter.

A strike vote was taken April 5th in protest of the election
held in October. Over 1000 employees walked out. We wore placards on
our hats and clothes indicating striker. A crew of forty-six police
had been sent to the strike district. They were friendly with us
strikers, and told us we were right in demanding our rights. Later
they changed their attitude when strikers clashed with "thugs" or strike
breakers imported by the company. These thugs carried ax handles,
hammers, and guns, which they used to threaten the strikers. In these
clashes our strikers were arrested and sent to jail for inciting a
riot. The thugs were hired to take the scabs to and from work. During this period, the chief of police placed a ban on picketing around
the mill. This lasted thirty-six hours. A temporary injunction was
obtained by our organizers restraining police from interference with
picketing strikers. They charged that police had interfered with
brutal force and unwarranted violence in preventing strikers from
picketing the vicinity of the mill.

During the strike the mill was running part time. This in-
fluenced some of our strikers to go back to work. Some were going in
every day, claiming they were losing their cars and homes. The situation became critical, and it looked as if we were going to lose our
strike. The case was taken to the National Labor Board where it was
finally settled. A contract was read to us at one of the mass meetings. We debated it from all angles, and agreed to accept it. The
settlement was not at all what we wanted; it seemed inadequate and

unjust, but it offered us the opportunity to get the whole mill organized when we returned to work. The proposition was worked out by representatives from both sides in Washington.

Under the terms of the contract the representatives of the union can deal with the management through the company union. All strikers are to be reinstated to their former jobs by applying in a body through the union and not as individuals. The National Labor Board will rule on any questions arising out of the application of the contract. The majority of the employees are now working. Seventy-five per cent of the black list group were reinstated.

I believe we have been successful to a certain extent. We can now deal with the management through our union. Wages have been slightly increased, and we have learned that where there is union there is strength.

COMPANY UNION

The day after the union organizers got in town, the company officials called a meeting of all employees in the shop. The purpose of this meeting was to organize a company union and throw all the mud on the labor union without giving it a showing. Not more than a dozen in the whole group had ever heard of the labor union, so naturally they voted for the side that was represented to them. Then the Yellow Dog contract was passed around and we were told to sign before we left.

Things moved on for a week or two. People were seen in corners whispering. Nobody said anything to you unless they knew which side you were on. Bitter resentment among the workers sprang up. Life long friendships were broken up. Your job and Friday afternoon's pay check were the key words.

The company union got the idea that they did not want to work in the shop with the labor union. They pulled a strike. The president of their union, who was the daughter of a foreman in the coat shop, guaranteed them that they would not be out more than two hours.

I arrived at the shop on that particular morning, and saw most of the employees huddled around the door. I looked the crowd over and immediately suspected what had happened. There were no cards on the clock; even the office crew were on the sidewalk. We demanded our cards and got them. At the appointed hour, we started work, but soon work ran out for some of us. "By Gad! punch the clock then. No, you can't do anybody else's work," was shouted at us.

About the middle of the morning, four uniformed policemen came walking up the stairs leading the strikers up. The group went over and cut the power off. A surprised hush fell over the building for a moment or two. The policemen did nothing; the foreman did nothing. What could we do? One boy picked up his shirts and started over there, but we stopped him. The odds were three to one against us and the cops were for the company.

The foreman's daughter could not back up her guarantee. They lost four hours. They got a contract that had no set time to expire or much of anything else. We, members of the labor union, were told that if we had any grievances to present, they would be brought through the company union committee which had signed the contract for the majority. We struck the following Monday.

In February, the Atlanta Regional Labor Board tried the owner for violation of the N.R.A. Our union won every point of the decision. The owner appealed the case to the National Labor Board. We won this decision. Then there were started a series of injunctions, until finally the Supreme Court ruled our perfect decision out of court with the sick chickens.

MY EXPERIENCES WITH A COMPANY UNION

I went to work at the F. Mills in 1921 when I was sixteen. There were about fifty other employees there, and since it was such a small group we all soon became very friendly. Mr. Higgins, one of the owners of the mill, would be around in the mill all day talking and laughing with us, telling each of us how important our particular job was and how much he personally depended on us to make "our mill" expand by producing a better product than any other hosiery mill in the country.

As the mill was enlarged and more people were hired, questions of conditions and higher rates began to come up. It was becoming exceedingly difficult for "J.A." to talk individually with his employees. So, at a very heavy expense to the company, he hired a new man from the East to come in and start an Employees' Representation Plan according to which the workers were to have equal rights with the owners. We were all working together for the best interest of all.

The employees in each department selected from their own members a "departmental director" whose duties were to settle disagreements between workers, carry complaints to the management, and in general represent the workers of the department. Problems of general concern were taken up in weekly meetings with the personnel manager, and if they could not be settled there they went to the Executive Board, composed of four workers elected by the workers, four representatives of management appointed by the manager, and the Personnel Director as chairman. Most of the problems that arose were settled to our satisfaction, and we were really "one big happy family." If we thought our wages were too low, we could have a time-study man check them. If our tables were too close or our lights not adjusted properly, our departmental director took care of that for us. As "all work and no play makes Jack a dull boy," our Executive Board planned basket and baseball teams, dances and picnics. We had group life insurance, sick benefits and a company doctor and nurse. What more could we ask for?

One day our departmental director came to us and asked us to sign a paper which carried this statement: "I will not join any outside union as long as I am an employee of the F. Mills." If one were not of legal age, he took it home and one of his parents signed it. (This is known as the double yellow dog contract.) We had signed those when we first went to work for the company, but they wanted to be sure the files were complete. We knew later that an organizer from the official union was in town at that time and our "J.A." wanted to be sure he was protected.

In 1925, our knitters had been complaining about low rates and long hours. They were told that business was bad and that the

company was losing so much money that they were lucky to have jobs.
This did not go over so big this time. Some of them got together
and said they would go on strike the next day if something was not
done. In less than an hour after this action was taken, we were all
told to leave our work and go over to the lunch room. "J.A." was
there looking as if he had lost his last friend. He began the meeting by telling us what a grand bunch of workers we were and how much
he thought of us, for we were as "dear to him as if we were his own
children." But now an "outside agitator" had come into town and told
"his boys" (the knitters) that the wages were higher and hours shorter in Philadelphia and Milwaukee. He said that this was not true,
and that the company was losing money every day. By the time he
finished this speech every man and woman was once again a member of
"the big happy family," and hours and wages were forgotten for the
time being.

Before long, however, our disagreements were so bad that the
departmental directors could not settle them. Our Executive Board always gave decisions in favor of the company. Several departments had
stopped work until they had received their demands, but the leaders
were always fired and the other workers did not dare fight.

In January, 1933, we began to organize in earnest. It was
a long hard job, for every one was afraid to let the next worker know
that he had signed up for the union. After the N.R.A. came into force,
we held our meetings in the open and elected our officers.

Our membership grew until in March, 1934, we had over 1000
workers signed up. Our conditions were steadily getting worse so we
decided to call a strike.

On April 6, 1934, about 1,800 workers came out on strike.
This left 1,700 in the mill. The strike was finally settled and almost all the workers got their jobs back. The most active ones, however were blacklisted. Those who were blacklisted went to the union
mills in Milwaukee and secured better jobs and higher wages. This
certainly defeated the aims of the company, for they hoped to use
this means to suppress further their employees. Instead, those workers came back to our union meetings, and told us how much better their
conditions were than ours. The rest of the strikers wished they had
been blacklisted.

Because of these and many other tactics of the company, the
workers in the F. Mills are at last waking up and joining a real trade
union. Some of them still have the "one big happy family" idea, but
even they are beginning to see that the head of the "family" must be
persuaded to recognize his responsibilities.

SHIRT-WORKER

My sister and I went down to the S. Tailoring Company and asked Mr. S. if he needed girls to work in his shop. He told us that he could not use us right then; but when he found out we had some experience with electric machines, he told us to come back in a day or two. We made three trips before he finally put us to work.

I began in the pants shop, putting in back pockets. After two weeks I was changed to vests where I made linings. I learned to be the fastest operator on that job and made $13 to $15 a week.

We started on the N.R.A. code about the time I was put on vests, but I did not get the $13.32 minimum wage until about four weeks later. We were paid by the piece. If we did not make the code, we got $13.32 anyway; and if we made more, we got that too.

I liked my work and got along fine with the floor lady and foreman. In the latter part of September, 1934, just after the general textile strike, two organizers came into our shop. They went around to some of the workers' homes and asked them to come to a union meeting that was to be held in a hotel. Word was passed around to a good many of the workers, and on Monday night about twenty were present. Among them were two boys, one a timekeeper and the other a work-carrier, whose sole purpose was to get all the information possible and report it to the bosses.

It was explained to us what the union stood for and some of the things you gained by the union. The next day a sign was posted on our clock to go up stairs to the coat department fifteen minutes before closing time for a special meeting of all employees. During the day, our timekeeper who had attended the meeting was out most of the day.

When we went upstairs for the meeting, the timekeeper gave a short talk about the meeting on the previous night, and his opinion of the organizers, which was not very good. Then he introduced the company union and told of its advantages. He said he believed everybody there would want to join and cooperate with Mr. S. He did not (nor did anyone get a chance to) explain what the labor union was. Several of the other company officials voiced their opinions in favor of a company union. Then ballots were passed out for voting on the company union or the labor union. The votes were counted, and about three times as many voted for the company union as for the labor union. Then sheets of paper were passed out requesting us to join no other union as long as we were in the employ of the company. We were asked to sign them before we left the building, and turn them back without fail.

LOSS OF MY JOB

After four and a half years working in a radio factory --
most of which time was spent in running an electric riveting machine, - I suddenly found myself out of a job. During the last
year of that period, work had become slack and the pay check
smaller and smaller. Finally it seemed as though there was little
use in working just to bring home a check of $8 or $10 for two
weeks' wages.

After a while, I discovered that some of the old girls
at the factory were working. I went back to find out why I also
could not do the same. When I reached the plant, I found that
they were hiring new girls, because under the N.R.A. the inexperienced girls could be paid 80 per cent of the minimum wage for experienced help. They would not rehire me, because they said my
work was too slow. It seemed queer that a concern should take
over four years to find out a person is inefficient in her work!

I asked about the stock I hold in the company. I was
told I could not get that either. This stock was issued a short
time before the N.R.A. came in. The method they used to get the
stock distributed to the employees was this: They called a meeting of all employees and told them the management was in need of
immediate funds. They then proceeded to explain to us how this
was to be done. The per cent taken from our check went according
to the amount of orders issued for the month. It usually amounted to about 10 per cent of our wages. Sometimes it was larger,
but it was never lower. We either had to take the stock, or we
would be out of work.

I went to the Industrial Commission to see if they would
be able to secure the stock for me, and was told I could not get
it at that time. I was told to consider it a cut in wages until
such time as business picked up, and they would be able to redeem
it.

TRADE UNIONS AND ORGANIZED SHOPS

HOW MY SHOP IS ORGANIZED

The Rochester Clothing plant in which I **work** has about 3,000 employees. Most of them are girls and women. In this plant we make men's clothing, consisting of suits and overcoats.

All the manufacturing departments of this factory are organized in the Amalgamated Clothing Workers of America and they have a trade union agreement with the firm. The factory is made up of many shops or departments, such as overcoats, sackcoats, pants and vests. In these shops the work is divided into many sections. Here are a few sections: Sleeves and off-pressers have their own section foreman, then the rest of the shop is divided up. The sackcoats shop is divided into eight sections in all. Each section has its own foreman who represents the firm. The union members of each shop elect their chairman, whose job it is to represent the workers. To show exactly how the factory is organized, I have drawn a chart.

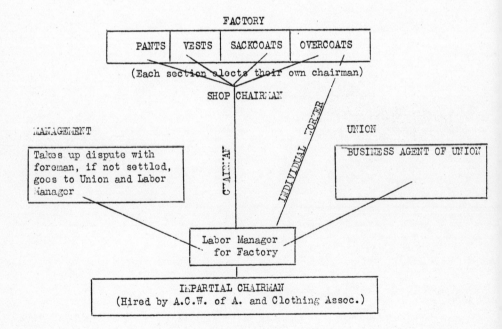

FACTORY

| PANTS | VESTS | SACKCOATS | OVERCOATS |

(Each section elects their own chairman)

SHOP CHAIRMAN

MANAGEMENT

Takes up dispute with foreman, if not settled, goes to Union and Labor Manager

INDIVIDUAL WORKER

CHAIRMAN

UNION

BUSINESS AGENT OF UNION

Labor Manager for Factory

IMPARTIAL CHAIRMAN
(Hired by A.C.W. of A. and Clothing Assoc.)

When a worker makes a complaint to the chairman, he takes
it up with the section foreman, and if he can not settle it satis-
factorily with the foreman, it is taken up with the Business Agent
of the Union, who in turn discusses it with the Labor Manager of
the firm. If these two can not agree, the matter goes to the Impartial Chairman for a final decision. The Impartial Chairman is
appointed by the firm and the union, and they both agree to abide
by his decision. Sometimes a dispute arises over a change in style,
which means that the operation has to be changed, and this takes the
operators longer. Because they are paid on a piece-work basis, they
want an adjustment in the price.

Division of work is another thing that often has to be
taken up. Sometimes a dispute may arise over a worker who is un-
fairly discharged, or who is charged for damaged work which is not
his fault. Because of the trade union agreement which the workers
in our industry have with the firm, any grievance of the worker or
difference of opinions can be adjusted. Through this cooperation
between the workers and the firm, better conditions exist in the
industry.

UNION ORGANIZATION IN THE CARPET INDUSTRY

The first Wilton carpet factory was located in Lowell, Massachusetts, in 1842. In later years the industry spread to New York, Connecticut, Pennsylvania and New Jersey. Philadelphia is the largest manufacturing center. Most Wilton carpet weavers came from Kidderminster, the carpet manufacturing center of England. The Wilton weavers were first organized in 1876, and in 1891 Wilton weavers were permanently organized with 100 per cent membership. This union lasted 30 years.

When the union was first formed, weavers received $9 for sixty hours a week. A fifty-five hour week was later gained by a general strike. From 1906 to 1912, improvements in working conditions and advances in wages were secured. At that time, weavers received $18 a week. That was not a uniform rate between the shops. As the result of a strike in 1912, the union secured forty-eight hours a week and a uniform price list. By this time every Wilton factory in Philadelphia, was organized. The carpet mills in other localities, however, were not organized until later. In 1915, there were 715 paid up members, all weavers; in 1919, 1540; in 1920, 1744. In 1920, there were locals in Worcester and Palmer, Massachusetts; Amsterdam, New York; Thompsonville, Connecticut; and Freehold, New Jersey. Each shop in Philadelphia had a local.

Wilton weavers controlled entrance to the trade by apprenticeship regulations and initiation fees. Apprentices to weaving had to be hired directly as helpers, creeler boys, altering boys or spare hands on the looms. They had to serve four years before their training of trade was completed. Youths serving three years occasionally had a chance to operate looms, when a weaver was taken ill. No one over seventeen years of age was hired to learn weaving. It took quite a few years, after they served four years of helping, before they were considered skilled weavers.

Shop committees handled all grievances in the shop. Workers divided the work equally, kept records of apprentices and arranged substitutes for weavers who were out sick. No weaver was allowed to work overtime, except for making samples and that time was limited to three weeks. Weavers were required to receive written instructions for making rugs and to measure the first length, to see if they were making it correctly. There were no fines or docking of pay, if carpet was spoiled. If any weaver was discharged, he could apply to the officials of the union to get reinstated. There were very few shop grievances or discharge cases to be settled. The union agreements ran six months, and no strikes could be called during the course of an agreement. There were very few strikes in the Wilton carpet mills.

In January, 1918, a strike was called and an increase of 15 per cent in wages was secured. In May, 1919, and April, 1920, a 45 per cent increase was secured. By that time, weavers earned between

$60 and $70 a week. In January, 1921, the employer proposed a wage reduction of 25 per cent. A strike was called and it lasted eight months, when weavers accepted a 20 per cent reduction. In 1922, conditions became worse, and a second strike was called in June, 1922. The workers lost the strike and the union, because one group that opposed the leaders went back to work.

The union never belonged to the American Federation of Labor. It was always an independent union, containing all highly skilled men. The dyers and loom fixers in the trade belonged to the United Textile Workers' Union.

After the weavers lost the strike, a company union was formed by the company. Everyone had to join. An efficiency man was brought in who caused a lot of dissatisfaction among the workers. Workers did not have much say about anything going on in the shop, and every person had to do what the manufacturer said. In 1923 wages increased 10 per cent, but in six months time this increase was taken away. In 1928 another reduction from 10 to 15 per cent was put into effect. The average skilled weaver was making $34 a week. By this time, old union members realized what a union meant and tried to reorganize. The work was getting scarce and reductions were being made. By this time, average skilled weavers received $20 a week. In 1930 wages were reduced from 10 to 40 per cent.

On January 5, 1931, 250 weavers called a strike against a reduction in wages and conditions. The reduction affected every department in the factory. No girls came until the winders and twisters received another 33 per cent reduction. Burlers did not come out until two days after that. Twenty-two burlers said they would come out when the time came, but only eight came out. The next day we visited the girls' houses. We tried to persuade them to come out, but they said they would not come until every one in the mill came out. In a few days we started on the picket line.

MY FIRST EXPERIENCE AS AN ORGANIZER

I came home from the lake, and the lady next door told me that two girls had been down to visit me. She did not know who they were, but they had left their cards in the mail box. When I looked on the names on the cards, the names did not look familiar. On the card was a telephone number that I should call between 10:00 and 11:00 o'clock. I dialed the number and discovered it was the office of a clothing union. I asked for Miss K., and she replied, "Speaking."

"This is G."

"Oh," she said, "When can you come down to see me?"

"I am working now but I can see you Saturday afternoon at 2:00 o'clock."

In the meantime, I was laid off. When I came to the union office, Miss K. asked if I were still working. I said, "I was laid off today."

Then she asked if I would take a job in one of the nearby pants factories. This was in a town about ten miles from X. Miss K. explained that in this town, the girls were not organized, and the union came out to organize a shop.

In this particular shop, the boss had fired one of the pressers because he had hung leaflets in the washroom. He went up the fire escape at 5:00 in the morning and climbed in the window. The heading of the leaflets was "Sweat Shops." They had union prices on one side and non-union prices on the other. The girls came in the washroom and read the leaflets. Two girls, who were always with the boss, came out and told him there were union leaflets in the washroom.

One of the girls in the shop, who was in contact with Miss K. told her that the bosses were going to have a Hallowe'en party for the girls. She promised Miss K. that she would take her. Miss K. asked if I would get a job and take the other organizer, Miss G., because they were sure they were going to have bosses from New York to speak against the union. I was to find out their names, and get information about how the boss treated the girls, and some of the girls' names. I told her I would, so we made arrangements with Miss G. for Monday morning.

We took the train then for X. After we got off the train we both separated. She walked on one side of the street and I on the other till we arrived at the factory.

Miss G. went on and I went in the factory. I waited fifteen minutes, and the janitor came along. He asked me what I wanted and I asked him if they were hiring experienced machine operators. He said,

"Yes, come on upstairs." He was excited. This was the first men's clothing shop in X., and very few girls were experienced on power machines.

I hesitated for a moment and thought I had better not go up. By the time we reached the second floor, I was so nervous I did not tell the story I had planned. I was to tell him I lived there and give my Lithuanian name; but when he asked me where I lived, I said in Y. He wanted to know why I did not try to get a job in Y. He said the girls did not make very much for a start. I told him I could not get a job in Y. I was going to live with friends in X.

He kept on saying that I better try to get a job in Y. He left me standing without saying whether he would hire me or not. Right in front of me was the pressing machine, on the right side of the presser were the bushelers. In back of the pressers were about ten rollers of machines.

There were ten girls besides myself waiting to be hired. Some would walk up to the girls working on the machine and watch how they worked, and some would teach them while they were waiting for the job. Some of the girls would walk in the washroom. I went in the washroom. I thought, "This would be a good chance to paste leaflets in the washroom." I would paste it on so well they would never get it off. When we came out, I asked a girl what they paid.

"Oh they don't pay much. You have to work the first week for nothing."

The boss came back about 10:00 and took me over to the foreman. The foreman started to question me and I told the same story. The girls would ask me where I was from. I would tell them. They would be so surprised and say, "You have to work one week for nothing, and all the carfare you have to pay!"

The boss would come around and take the time. If he saw that a girl had made more than $7 the rates were lowered per hundred.

The second day, a girl came up to me and asked if I lived in Y. and asked my name. I told her my first name. She said she thought I had said I lived in Y. She kept on rubbing it in that we were just working for nothing.

At 12:00 the machinery stopped, and Elsie called me to have lunch with her. We started to talk about the wages and she said, "Some girls from New York were here and tried to organize; but you know you can't organize the Italians, they don't stick together."

"What makes you think that?"

"Why Rita, the short thin girl over there is the girl who squealed about the leaflets. Isn't it just like the dumb workers not to stick together?" Then the whistle blew and we started to work.

Later in the afternoon, Helen came around and asked if I would like to go to a Hallowe'en party, "and it will cost 50 cents." The boss came up to Helen and said, "We will have to postpone the party."

"What for?"

He said, "Therez a r-r-reason for it."

"Why we have costumes ready."

"I dunt care. But therez a r-r-reason, the bosses can't come."

"As if we cared whether they came or not," we said to ourselves. But finally we persuaded him to let us have an informal dance.

Every time the boss would give me a new lot to sew, he would make about two pairs of pants before he would let me sew. Once he came up to me and said, "What's the matter that you don't sew faster?"

"Why, don't I sew fast enough?"

He said, "Get up, let me sew. No wonder," he said, "your machine is slow." Then he tightened the belt and made a few pairs of pants. I laughed to myself, "He must be worried I wasn't going to make anything."

Next morning he was talking to the girl next to me and telling about a wrist watch that his girl gave him. Then he came to me and started to talk and asked me if I would like to be his girl. I told him, "What about the girl that gave you the wrist watch?"

"I was kidding the girls. I don't have a girl."

He was very untidy about himself, and chewed tobacco and let the saliva run down the side of his mouth. He asked my name and I told him G. He said, "O! that's a long name. I'm going to call you Jean." I laughed at him. He went on, "You know it's a rule not to pay the girls the first week, but I like you, and I'm going to pay you the first week." When I came home from work I told my sister about it and said, "I don't know if I should feel flattered or insulted."

Miss K. and two other organizers came up that evening and asked how I made out at work. I told her about Helen, the girl that watched me every time I had to pass by her, and the two spies, Rita and Mary, and gave her a description of the two girls. I told her that the plans of the Hallowe'en party were changed to an informal dance without masks and so we could not go. I also told her about the boss, how he would swear and call the girls names, and about the

girls comparing their prices with the union and saying how much more
they would make if they had a union.

Next day I had to go back to my old job. When I went back
to the pants factory the next Monday, the boss wanted to know why I
had not called him up. I told him I had to get glasses. He said he
had hired a new girl and as much as he liked me, he had had to let
me go. He paid me when I was leaving. The girls snickered as I
passed by.

I went down to the union office, the girls asked what was
the matter and I told them I was fired. They made a big joke of it.
It was the first time I had been fired.

Helen, from the shop, called up Miss K. and told her that
the girls had put the blame on me for getting their names and address-
es and sending them leaflets, and the boss had fired me./

WHY MY BOSS ENCOURAGED THE UNION

For over a year and a half, the union had been trying to organize our shop, which employs about 400 workers. On this particular morning, we heard that a few of the girls had received pamphlets concerning the prices in union and non-union shops. Naturally we girls had become curious, and wanted to compare our prices with the union prices. During lunch hour my girl friend and I decided to investigate. It did not take us long to find a few of these pamphlets, and to read them without the boss seeing them, as we thought, but found out different later. Well everything went fine until about 2:30, when I noticed my girl friend come out of the office, pass me and give me a wink, which meant, "Trouble ahead, Kid."

Sure enough, a few minutes later I was in the office. This is what I went through for the next hour or so. Mr. Boss said to me, "How long have you been working here?"

"I said, "Four years."

He then asked. "You like to work here?"

Well, I was working in the shop, and naturally I had to say "Yes."

He then asked, "Did you get paper or letters from S. lately?"

"No, not that I know of."

"Are you sure? Now think."

Although I was scared stiff, I still can not figure out where I got the nerve to give him my telephone number, and to tell him to call my sister up if he did not believe me. In the meantime, I had gotten mail, which I found out about when I came home that evening. Supposing he had called up, what a fine pickle I would have been in!

But he finally said, "Have you seen any mail about the shop about some kind of a union or something of the sort?"

"Yes, not only one but several."

"Why didn't you show them to me?"

"Why should I? If they wanted you to see them they would send you a copy."

"What do you think about the union?"

"I think it's a good thing, but I don't think it would work out so well in this shop."

"Why?"

"Because there are too many kids working between the ages of fourteen and sixteen who would be afraid of being fired."

"Would you join if they started a union?"

"Surely, why not, if it is going to help me get better wages and conditions? I think I should try and help make it a good strong union."

He then sat back and looked at me with his big eyes, for about five minutes, which seemed like an hour. We have given him a name, Eagle Eyes, because whether he was looking at you or not he would always see what you were doing. Then he said, "Uh-huh," and kept looking at me. Really my heart was in my throat, but the Good Lord must have given me courage to speak to him the way I did. So he finally asked for a copy of the pamphlet or to show him a girl that had one. I told him I was no squealer, which he did not like a bit. He told me he would fire me if I joined the union, or did not show him the girl. My brother was working steady at the time. I figured he would be able to support me; so I said, "O. K., if that's the reason for firing me, all right." But here I am still in the same factory.

A few days later, my friend had some work to do beside me. When we looked at each other, she winked and said, "Keep mum, we are being watched." She no sooner got through talking, when the big shot's brother, Joe, came down, separated us, and put his nephew George in between us, so anything we had to say could be heard by George. He never figured, though, that we were able to talk in Polish, which we often did. So George was not a great help, after all.

About three months later, a man from the union came into our shop, and told us to join the union, with the boss' consent. The next day we received little slips to sign our membership into the union. Nobody signed but one girl, and we made her erase her name. We felt that just because the boss said we were to sign, we would not.

That afternoon the boss stopped me as I was walking with a group of girls, and asked me if I had signed to join the union. I said, "No. If I had joined the union before, I would have been fired. If I do not join now, I am fired. What am I supposed to do, read your mind?"

He then began telling me we had to join the union in order to get work from New York and other manufacturers, because union truck drivers and union textile manufacturers and union cutters in New York were keeping their materials from being delivered into a non-union shop. So the following day we were all union members, whether we wanted to be or not, with a 10 per cent increase in pay.

Although we were forced into the union and have the checkoff system in paying our dues, we are getting along wonderfully, and looking forward to a 20 per cent increase in pay in a very short time.

MY BOSS

One fine Saturday morning, I came to work and found all the girls sitting at their machines, but not working. A stoppage. They soon informed me that they had not been able to agree on prices the evening before, and had decided not to start work until the boss came to terms.

In the meantime, the price committee was in the office arguing the case. A few minutes later, one of the committee came out to ask for reinforcements. The boss had made an offer, and they wanted more girls to be present while the bargain was made. I agreed to go in.

In the showroom stood Mr. S. - short, lean and dark. He had a Charlie Chaplin moustache, and high cheek bones. He was in his shirt sleeves, and his hands played nervously with the gold chain which was hanging across his vest. His beady eyes were running from one object to another, and did not seem to be able to focus on any one thing. Presently he began to talk across the table to the committee, and while talking he made violent motions with his short arms to prove his point.

"You girls are running me out of business. You know as well as I do that I can't pay more than 85 cents a dress. In fact I am losing money as it is. You know yourselves that this is not the busy season. I didn't have to cut this lot. It is not an order; it's stock. I may not even be able to sell it. But I am doing it for your sakes - to keep you busy." And then in a softer tone of voice, and slowly, "After all, if I don't look out for you, who\will?"

After delivering this smooth piece of oratory, he paused, smiled benevolently, and assumed a confident air as if to say, "If that doesn't please them, I don't know what will."

But the committee, having heard this line of argument before, refused to be taken in by it. They explained that they were authorized to take no less than 90 cents for the garment.

Such audacity! Mr. S. grew furious. His face turned purple with rage; his small eyes became red and almost bulged out of their sockets. His whole body quivered and leaned forward like an animal before jumping on its prey.

He finally controlled himself somewhat, let his fist down on the table with all his might, and yelled at the top of his voice, "You may tell the girls that they can sit there from now until Doomsday; they will not get another nickel."

The following Monday the junior partner of the firm arrived and agreed to give us the nickel. We went back to work. But the boss took his revenge by insisting that there be a new price committee.

I GET A JOB IN A UNION TOBACCO FACTORY

I had been trying to get work for about two weeks, when my father told me he had heard that the P. Tobacco Company was hiring girls. I went down to the factory and applied. After a few questions I was told to report on Monday.

The girls were nice, but not very talkative, and I was too modest to begin conversation. I was there a week before the feeling of being new began to leave me, and I started to talk more with the girls. There were 125 girls employed there, and they all belonged to the union.

After working there two weeks I was asked to join the union. The reason I had to wait was that the officials of the company would select the girls they wanted to keep, and then the union would approve them. I was initiated at the next union meeting.

The girls are as a rule a very cooperative group, but of course sometimes they have petty grievances, such as the question of seniority rights. The most frequent grievance is that of the infringement of seniority rights; that is, the girl who is there the longest receives promotion first. Often times, however, the boss tries to advance a girl out of turn, with the result that the girl who should have been promoted goes to the grievance committee about it where the matter is soon settled. A girl must work in the shop a year before she receives seniority rights.

I had never come in contact with the active working of the union, until one day we ran out of union labels. Each package of tobacco going out must have a union label, and as soon as the last one was used we stopped the machines. The boss came into the shop all excited and wanted to know what was wrong. When we told him the labels were all used, he pretended he knew nothing of it, and asked us if we would not consider staying and working without them the remainder of the day, in order to fill the orders. We would not accept the proposition. We decided to go home, and when we reported to work the next morning we had the union labels.

Besides the every day disputes which had come up and are settled by the committee, we have to negotiate our wage scale which expires every five years. The boss is also doing some planning for that; he collects price circulars from the chain stores to give us the idea that the price of food, etc., is going down. The committee points out to the boss that the costs are also going down, and that the owner's profits are still the same, while the price of tobacco is still the same.

For the same wage scale, the company tried to take seniority rights from us, but the committee would not give in and we still have our seniority rights. It seemed that for every negative argument the boss put up, the committee had a positive answer, and so we retained our old wage scale without much trouble or strike.

THE CLOSED SHOP

I had worked for my firm for fourteen years and made good
money. I made an average of $25 per week, on finishing coats. I
quit when work became slack in order to take a vacation, and I stayed out for a year and a half until August, 1932, when work began to
pick up. When I got back to work I was not put on my regular job but
on another, so that with the prices cut down as they had been during
the depression I could not make more than $9 or $10 a week. Although
my work was satisfactory during the fourteen years I had worked there
as well as since August, 1932, when I went back with the firm, I
could not make more than this.

In June, 1933, the N.R.A. came along, and the minimum wage
in our code was set at $12. Along with the majority of operators in
our shop, I could not quite make it. We had to keep a time sheet on
which we marked up just the hours and minutes we served. The firm
hired a timekeeper to go over the shop and mark the hours on our sheets
with pen an ink. The boss would call up everyone who could not make
the minimum and bawl them out. He would tell them that if they wanted
their job they had better make their hours and tickets average. He did
not call me at all because my average had gone up.

When we started under the N.R.A. I made 21 cents to 26 cents
per hour. One day the timekeeper said to me, "You were not at your
machine when I came by yesterday morning, and you have eight hours
marked up." I said, "I know it. I had gone over to put my bundle on
the table."

She went on. In a few minutes, the boss came over and asked
me if I had made eight hours any day that week. I said, "Yes." I
asked why, but he said nothing and went on. I sewed for a few minutes,
but I got madder and madder. I said, "I'm going over and take my time
sheet and show it to him." I did and he said, "No operator could make
eight hours in one day, because they are always going to the dressing
room and so on." I said, "Well, when I start to work at 7:45 and work
until 4:30 I'm going to mark up eight hours just the same." He told
me he was going to investigate it and I said, "O.K. go ahead. I have
not lied about it."

The next afternoon, which was the day we turned in our time,
the floor lady came around and told me the boss wanted to see me when
I finished the bundle I was working on. I went to see the boss. He
told me he wanted to lay me off. I said, "O.K., but first I want to
know why you are laying me off." He said my average was not coming up
as it should. I know it was, so I said, "Let us go see my time card."
We did and I had gone from 21 cents to 26 cents per hour. I said, "You
just said my average had not gone up as it should." All he could say
was, "That was the order from the office." I asked him for the time so

that I could take it to the office. He finally gave it to me, and I
went to the general manager with it. I told him that the superintendent was laying me off because of my average; I handed him my card and
pointed out how it had gone up. He asked me how long I had worked
there and I said, "Fifteen years." "Well," he said, "the office has
decided to lay off all old operators who can't make the minimum. We
can't afford to pay money out to you like that." I said, "O.K., but
I would like to have this card." He told me that that was company
property.

"Very well," I said, "I have a copy of all my time sheets
and my pay envelopes." I went back to the workroom and took it to
the chairman of our shop committee, who was appointed through the
union. She went to our president and then to the boss. I am sorry
to say that neither of them talked for me at all. In fact I think
they would have talked against me had I not been there. They were
more in favor of the firm. However, when I finished all I had to
say, and the boss had finished saying what he wanted to, he told me
he was not going to lay me off. He told two other girls who were
laid off at the same time that he would have to let them go as they
were hopeless.

I got my job back, and have been working over since. Although he did not say so at the time, I think the reason he wanted
to lay me off was because I was an active member of my local. But
he would be headed for trouble if he had laid me off: we have a
closed shop.

WORK IN A UNION SHOP

In 1922, I went to work in a union factory where overalls, pants and children's play suits were made. This building was large, with plenty of space, well lighted and ventilated with windows, comfortably heated in winter and with very modern conveniences for the workers.

This was a union factory, which meant that I was paid better wages, worked shorter hours, and had better working conditions than when I worked in an open shop. The superintendent told me that after I had worked three weeks I would be admitted into the union, thus giving me time to decide whether or not I would stay on the job.

The superintendent assigned me to a felling machine. The first week I made $12.50. After working a while, I soon found that I did more work and did it with greater ease, working eight hours per day than I had done before in ten hours, and was paid more and was not nearly so tired after my day's work. After I had been there a week or two, I decided that the machine was rather high for me, and when I mentioned this the machinist had my treadle and chair raised, which was a great help to me.

I have been working here for many years, and have made $30 a week. Since the depression, orders have been slow in coming in, and I have been working only two and three days a week. But I have had no wage cuts.

THE BANANA ARGUMENT

While working in an organized dress factory, I was elected chairlady. It was my duty to set the prices of each style with the managers or employer. On one style we could not agree. The operators told me they wanted $6 for making a particular dress, and the manager wanted to pay $4.50. When I came to the workers and told them about it, they were indignant and refused to consider the offer. The manager then came over to the machines and spoke to the workers.

"It is the duty and to the interest of the workers to see that the employer does good business; otherwise how will you be employed? If you demand such high prices, how can your employer sell his merchandise and compete with other firms?" And, pointing to me, he said: "This woman evidently wants to live on Riverside Drive and go to Broadway shows, so she tries to get high wages. We ought to know better than to live above our means. We are workers, and we have to live where rent is cheap and food is cheap. Of course, where our boss lives, one banana costs a nickel, but where I live I get two bananas for a nickel. I am sure that on First Avenue, where most of you live, you can get beautiful fresh bananas four for a nickel, and that goes for everything else we need."

Strange as it may seem, his words had the effect he knew they would. When I indignantly protested against his arguments, the workers told me that we ought to consider what he said, as there was a lot of truth in it. Of course I went to the union, and came back with instructions to shut the power off and to go to a meeting with our delegate. The workers refused to stop, and told me they had already settled the price with the manager. I had an awful time thereafter, and the manager made it impossible for me to remain.

WE WON!

"So you went and made a complaint to the Union! Well, I'll fix you, you little rat!" yelled the boss at R.

R. blanched, but stood her ground. The other girls cowered and kept very still. The anger of the boss was terrible to see. They looked at each other and wondered what R. would do.

"I've a right to complain to the Union," she said quietly.

This seemed to anger the boss, for he yelled louder than ever, "You little skunk, you're fired! Get out! Get out!"

All work had ceased in the shop. Everybody was watching the scene. Now what would happen?

"You have no right to fire me. You've got to make a complaint to the Union and give a specific reason why," answered R. as calmly as she could. She turned back and continued her work.

The boss glared and sputtered, got red in the face, and looked as if he was ready to murder the calmly working girl. He finally turned and ran to the phone, grabbed it with such a jerk that he knocked it off the table. He yelled into the speaker for the Union office. Finally getting it, he started pouring out a torrent of words to the manager and threatening to lock out all the workers. The manager told him to calm down and he would come over and see what the trouble was. As the boss turned from the phone, everybody started to work furiously, striving not to get in his way. He went around swearing and growling and calling all the girls skunks and rats and little louses who just ate their way into the boss's bones.

The manager finally arrived with the bosses' association representative. They called R. and went into the office. The girls whispered among themselves, "If he gets R. out, he'll do the same to all of us. I hope she wins."

Moments passed; the girls became fidgety and more worried. Finally R. came out beaming, walked to her table, and started to work.

The workers had won that time!

HOW TO GET BETTER WAGES

I had been working in this shoe factory for about four years. I was doing what they called tongue stitching. This factory is a union shop; and when we get new patterns we always get new prices from our forelady. Then, if we think that the price is not right, we talk it over with the forelady and tell her that we can not make anything on that price. She usually looks it all over, and then raises the price if she thinks it is too low.

One day I got a new pattern which was similar to the pattern that I was getting 11 cents a dozen for. When I went to get my price for the new pattern, the forelady handed me a piece of paper which read 8 cents a dozen. I took it with me to my machine and stitched a dozen tongues to see how much I could make. I knew when I received the new price that I could not make anything, but I thought I would give it a fair trial. So I stitched a dozen and found out I could not make more than 30 cents an hour. I took the price slip back to the forelady and told her that the price was too low. She took the price slip and picked up one of the shoes. She measured the stitches and looked at the price, finally telling me that that was the best she could do. So I told her that I would not stitch another of this pattern.

This happened on a Monday, the day that our Union man collects our dues. It was just about 11:30 A.M. when the Union man got to my machine. By this time there was about 200 pairs of tongues at my machine which they were waiting for, but I would not stitch any for the price was too low. When the Union man saw all the work at my machine, he asked what was the trouble. I showed him the new price I got for the new work, and told him that I would not stitch any for that price. He took the price slip and said he would see what he could do about it. I could see him talking with the forelady, who was still shaking her head. Then I saw him use the phone.

It was about ten minutes after 12:00 when everything was quiet and the girls were all eating their dinner that I saw the forelady, the Union man and the superintendent coming toward my machine. I stopped eating my dinner, for I just did not know what was going to happen. When they did get to my machine, the Union man asked me, "How much do you think that this pattern is worth?" I said, "At least 11 cents like my other work. Although this pattern may have less stitching, the work on it is much harder." Then the superintendent asked the forelady if she thought that was right. She still insisted that this pattern was much easier than my old patterns. By this time, I was getting good and sore. All eyes in the place were on us and everything was so quiet. Then I asked the forelady if she would sit down and try to stitch a shoe. She did not like this so she replied that she had done this job before she became forelady. I replied that this was years ago. When she heard that she turned and looked at the Union man and the superintendent and shook her

head and said that the price was all right. By this time her face was
as red as a beet. She walked away and the superintendent followed her.
Then the Union man asked me if I was going to stitch the work after
what I heard. I said, "No, I'd rather go home than to sit there and do
that work." So then he told me to eat my dinner, that he would see me
after dinner hour. At 3:00 that afternoon, the forelady handed me a
slip of paper which read 12 cents for the new pattern, but she would
not even speak to me. I really thought that I was going to be fired
after the way I talked to her, but now she speaks to me much better
now than she did before. Now any time I get a new pattern, and I think
that the price is too low, she always asks me why do I think so. Then
we talk it over until we come to some agreement.

When the girls found out that I got the price I asked for,
they all wanted to know how I did it. I told the girls that they just
have to fight for their rights and they would get them.

REINSTATING A WORKER ON HER JOB

The garment shop, where this incident occurred, was a union shop. It was owned by a father, two sons, and a son-in-law. The designer, who did some of the work-room managing, made a fifth boss. Sometimes they would try to out-boss each other. At such times it was woe for us, because we could not determine who was the boss, and whose orders we should carry out. The operators worked on a piece-work basis.

One morning we came to work, as we were told to by one of the bosses. But the work was not ready, and we had to wait in the shop until it was ready. This was one result of having too many bosses in one factory.

M., who got tired of waiting at her machine, went over to speak to the draper, who was a friend of hers. The draper was a time-worker. When the designer saw M. speaking to the draper, he told her to go away. He had to speak to her a second time, and this started an argument. One of the bosses happened to be around, and he wanted to know what it was all about. The designer told him that M. had been talking to E. ever since she came in, and he had told her fifteen times to leave her alone. Instantly M. rebelled at the false accusation and called him a "liar."

I was at that time the shop chairlady and on the price committee. I also had charge of the equal division of work. When a cutter would get through with a cut, he would bring it to me and I would divide it equally among the operators. I kept a list, so that if a girl got less work one week, she would get more the next week to make up for what she had lost the previous week.

When the designer got through arguing with M., he came over to me and told me not to give her any more work; that she was through. I told him I would continue to give M. work until I got official orders not to.

When the cutter brought over the work to me, I divided it as usual among the girls. As soon as I got through, the designer took M.'s work and carried it off, basket and all. That caused a commotion among the girls. I got up and went to the office to look for one of the bosses. I found all four of them in the show-room adjoining the office. I told them the story and they said they had nothing to do with it. Mr. L. was taking charge of that department. I reminded them that the union had an agreement with them and not with the designer. They kept quiet. I understood that they liked Mr. L. very much and could not very well go against him.

I felt something had to be done to reinstate M. If not, the designer might make a practice of getting rid of girls in such

a manner. And before we would know it, we would all be out of there.
I went back to the girls and told them my opinion. They felt the same
about it.

During lunch hour, I went down to our union office and told
our manager. I insisted upon his going back with me to the shop.
When we got there, we went into the office and called in the designer
in the presence of the bosses, which made five against two.

After a long discussion, the designer finally admitted that
he had exaggerated a bit when he said he had spoken to her fifteen
times, but that still he was not a liar, as she had called him. And
it was decided that M. should go back to work.

M. had not known what was going on at all. She had left
the shop when the work was taken away from her. Suddenly she came
back, and into the office for her pay, for this happened to be pay
day. When the designer saw her, he said to us jokingly, "If she'll
promise to behave herself and apologize to me, I might let her come
back." M., who was a bit quick tempered, turned round with her big
sparkling black eyes flaring at him, and said, "What, me apologize
to you? I should say not. Why, I wouldn't work for you if I had to
starve." She walked out just as suddenly as she had entered.

For a moment I stood there dumfounded. I felt like saying,
"Well done, M.," because he deserved it. He used to say much more to
some of the girls, and got away with it. I was waiting for the designer to speak. And after a tense moment which seemed like an age, he
said that he would not take her back. "She is too proud." I told him
that we all have a right to our own pride. And after another long dispute, M. was reinstated.

HOW THE CHAIRMAN OF OUR LOCAL WAS REINSTATED

The day at the shop had been a strenuous one for me; it seemed that on this particular day we had more petty grievances to present to the superintendent than at any time since the day we had organized and presented our demands. All day I had an uneasy feeling that there was trouble brewing in the air and that something was bound to happen before the night shift would close at 4:15 A.M.

The men were fighting for a forty-eight hour week instead of the fifty-five hour week they had been working on since before and after the strike. The chairman of the General Committee was told that he would receive an answer at 9:00 that evening, for Mr. L. the owner was out of town and would not be back until then.

About 5:00, the chairman was called to the Superintendent's office and was told that Mr. L. could not see how he could get the same amount of production in forty-eight hours, and still give the workers their 10 per cent bonus. Mr. L. would have to think the matter over until payday, which was only three days off, when he would give them his answer definitely. There was also another message from Mr. L., saying that one of the officers of the union would receive a slip of paper stating that his services would not be needed any longer.

Right after supper the chairman came down to see me, and stated that it was up to us officers and the members of the union to put a stop to this dismissal before it was done. This was the first weapon Mr. L. was trying to use to disorganize us and form a company union.

After we had discussed the situation thoroughly, we called the president of the Central Labor Union up on the phone and explained to him our troubles. He replied that he would come down to the house immediately. When he arrived, he advised us to telephone the organizer right away, which we did. The organizer told us to call a special meeting Wednesday at 4:15 P.M. for both day and night shifts.

When our chairman returned to work, the foreman handed him an envelope, which bore the following message: Your services after today will not be required any longer. We find, that we, the undersigned, have not the necessary work to keep you busy. This was signed Mr. L.

The news spread like wild fire, and immediately the entire night shift knew what had happened. Right away protests were made, that unless he were reinstated within the next twenty-four hours the workers would refuse to go back to work again.

The mass meeting started with a perfect attendance - not one person went back to work that night on the 4:15 P.M. shift. The workers were all waiting for action.

We appointed a committee of five to see Mr. M., the superintendent, and demand reinstatement of our chairman. Mr. M. said he could not reinstate him at all. We pleaded and pleaded with Mr. M. to call Mr. L. up, which he finally consented to do. The minutes and seconds seemed eternity, and then the blow came - Mr. L. refused to reinstate our chairman.

The members took the news very calmly, and the question was put up to them, as to what they intended to do about this situation. One of the members got up and asked for the floor. He said that we, as brothers and sisters, should stick to one another through thick and thin, and that this was the time to strike until our chairman was reinstated. All the members agreed with him.

The news spread that the C. weavers were out on strike again. At 10:00, the same committee went back, and told Mr. M. that we had struck, and the reasons why.

Mr. M. immediately called up Mr. L., and told him what had happened. He pleaded with Mr. L. to reinstate the chairman. He told Mr. L. that we had enough trouble during the last strike, and if the workers walked out again the shop would lose orders.

Mr. L. asked if we would always walk out if some member were fired, and we all yelled over the mouthpiece, "Yes." He finally gave in and said, "Yes," and not too graciously either.

And so our chairman was reinstated, and a complete victory was won in one night.

MY EXPERIENCE AS HALL CHAIRMAN

My activities as shop chairman caused my discharge from one
of the biggest department stores in a middle western city. The officials of my local of the White Goods Workers' Union, assigned me the
Hall Chairmanship during the strike scheduled to be called one week
later. Having been instrumental, along with two other members, in
organizing the shop, I felt inestimably proud when 312 girls out of
365 registered at the hall on the day of the walkout.

With the help of union officials, I had procured all the necessary equipment, such as banners named for the different shops to be
picketed, strings and large pins, and had formed a committee to see
that these banners were comfortably adjusted before the girls left the
hall. Street car tokens were available to those who had long distances
to travel to reach their designated factories. A clerical department
was set up so that the union knew exactly which factory each girl was
picketing, and at what hour of the day.

A most important part of my duties was to arrange a commissary.
We built a substantial kitchen with shelves and cupboards to house the
pots and pans and crockery necessary in cooking to satisfy the needs of
a hungry crowd. A second-hand stove was installed, donated by the
mother of the secretary of the local. Two of the strikers very efficiently took charge of the cooking. Rolls and coffee were obtainable
from 7:00 A.M. throughout the day. At noon a hot lunch was provided
consisting of beef stew, sometimes chilli, or chop suey, or roast lamb,
with vegetables and a variety of sandwiches on the side. During the
rest periods in the hall, the girls were cheered by lively entertain-
ments. Led by the orchestra, the whole mob would sing labor songs.

The workers had come to realize how dependent upon each other
they were for the protection of their labor rights, and together they
fought like demons. The police were very brutal to our girls, striking them in the face with batons, tripping them up, and using filthy
language. The girls resented this last more than anything else. They
would discuss their grievances on returning to the hall, and the sympathy gained from each other would encourage them to more determined
efforts the next day.

The paddy wagon was a standing joke. To be taken for a ride
was the greatest honor conferred on a striker. The girls all vied for
this honor, for great was the rejoicing when they returned from the
police station. On one occasion, six girls were put in the wagon and
taken to the station. During the ride, it was discovered that in the
confusion a strike-breaker had been dragged in by mistake. This close
and friendly proximity to a scab was more than our girls could endure.
They set about tearing her hair and dragging off her clothes. Finally
the police stopped the wagon and deposited her, with some of her clothing in her arms, on the sidewalk.

Eventually the manufacturers obtained injunctions against the union, restricting the pickets to three and thereby curbing the activities on the line. But the union had not been idle. Several hearings had taken place before the National Labor Relations Board. At one, all the strikers attending conclusively proved that we had walked out in a majority. A communication from Washington stated that an election was unnecessary, and that within ten days negotiations must be started between the department store and the organization chosen by the workers to represent them. This news created great jubilance among the strikers, but it was short-lived. The very day that the meeting had been arranged between the lawyers, the Supreme Court ruled the N.R.A. unconstitutional.

Most of the strikers were sent to work in union shops. Those remaining in the hall continued to picket the shop.

ON THE JOB

When I was offered my job as Business Agent some years ago, I took it with great reluctance. I had joined the waitresses' union when working in a restaurant in a department store, and had been fired for doing so. I was out of work, but I hesitated before taking a job with such responsibility.

I took this job as Business Agent of the Waitresses' Union with many misgivings. On Monday morning I started on my duties assured by the Business Agent of an affiliated men's union of his help and advice. With this hope, I entered his office.

"Well, I see you are on the job," he said. "What do you think you should do first?"

"I came here," I replied timidly, "supposing you would tell me a little of what my duties would be."

"You will visit the various restaurants," he said, as he busied himself with the mail before him. "Talk to the waitresses and try to get them to come into the union."

"Well, what shall I say to them. What argument may I use?"

"Use your own argument," he answered. "You'll have to learn by hard knocks how to get them in."

I started out on my journey filled with mixed emotions. I wondered where I would go first. I had an impulse to run away, because I felt that with no more definite ideas I simply could not go and talk to the girls. I went into a restaurant, approached a girl and asked her to join the union. She looked at me and said, "Aw! what d' I want t' join the union for? Hain't no good." She walked away.

I felt like going through the floor. My heart sank. How little I know! Tears came to my eyes, and I hurried out to walk along the street talking to myself. After many similar attempts, I finally learned how to talk to girls, how to persuade them to join the union for their own good. After many experiences, disappointments and discouragements, I saw our union grow.

After about six months came the question of a raise in wages, betterment of conditions and reduction of working hours. The union members had to agree upon what increase they would ask, and after days of argument the agreement was ready to be presented to the employer.

We found a man who refused to give the raise, although he had stated that he had made a profit and that his business was a pay-

ing institution. Every effort having failed to bring about a settlement, the inevitable strike came.

I shall never forgot the bitterness and suffering of that
my first strike! I had to be on the picket line to encourage and
oversee the others. As we walked up and down, men and women would go
into the restaurant; and as they passed us they offered insult after
insult until we wanted to scream and strike someone. But we always
had to be careful, for there was the law to protect the employer and
the public. A woman started into the restaurant. She stopped, looked at me contemptuously, and said, "You ought to be home, washing
clothes instead of here hurting this poor man." I could not stand it
any longer, and I answered her back. Then, the long arm of the law
reached me, stuck me into the patrol wagon, and then into jail. After
weeks of struggle, this employer agreed to settle, and every one went
back to work. I had to go on to the next task.

The tasks of a Business Agent are many and varied. In the
course of a day, I am called upon to meet many different situations.
A girl comes to me crying. Her baby is sick, but she cannot quit
work for the baby needs food and medicine. I have to help her, find
care for the baby, and encourage her to keep up her spirit. Then,
some girl has a grievance against her employer, and I must iron it
out. A girl quits her job, and I must find her another if possible,
and fill the place she left.

I have the union books to keep, the dues to collect, the
treasury to watch, and social affairs to manage. I must keep my
union on the map by telling every other union that we are organized,
and by reminding them to eat in union restaurants.

I close my desk at the end of the day, and wend my way home-
ward to my family feeling happy that I shall have a few hours rest
that night. I get myself all comfortable when the telephone rings.
Someone says, "Jennie Smith was badly scalded in the kitchen and we
have sent her to the hospital." I wearily dress, hurry to Jennie,
see her cared for, and then fill the place she has just left. I drag
myself home again, wondering, "What next?"

OUR GARMENT WORKERS' UNION

I am a member of Local #213 and I am going to tell you about
our campaign for membership.

Our organization is in its infancy, and far from being complete. At one of our meetings we decided it was necessary to form some
plan whereby we might get the workers interested in joining the union.
Our first plan was that each member should become an organizer; that is,
he should try to get someone else on the outside to join. Each member
was to work on one prospect a week.

While a few were brought in this way, for the most part we only
got promises. We decided to try another plan. Committees of three were
appointed to visit other organizations to ask their help, for most all
of the members of the carmen, carpenters, plumbers, bricklayers, printers and railroad unions have wives, sisters and sweethearts working in
our factories. Our plan was to get these men who knew so well what it
means to be organized to interest these women in our garment workers'
union, by explaining to them what it would mean to them in the way of
higher wages, better working conditions and more freedom.

We had some success from this plan, but we were not satisfied
with results. Our next plan was to collect 5 cents from each member of
all the different locals and buy a set of silverware to be given away
at a mass meeting. We advertised the meeting on the cards we had
printed with duplicate numbers to be drawn at the meeting. The one
holding the lucky number would be the winner. Of course we had our
speakers. The fact that something was to be given away free, drew
quite a large crowd. After the drawing and speeches, we had eighteen
new members, and fifteen new applications for membership. We tried
this plan twice with very good success.

At another time we gave a social (in fact we do this once a
month now). We have music, dancing, speakers and refreshments. The
speakers are sometimes from a railway union, the printers' union. The
president of our Federation of Trades has spoken, and once we had some
of our own members speak. We have had some real encouragement here.
We have new members drifting in every week.

Our last plan has been to have printed on handbills the union
schedule of prices, and the men from our Federation of Trades each week
stand at the door of our plant and hand out these bills to the workers
as they come out. This has caused the company quite a bit of concern
and they have tried to have it stopped, but can not.

We are now expecting an international organizer, and have hopes
of keeping him until we are 100 per cent organized and can demand a contract with our boss. We hope to sit across the table from him and see
him sign on the dotted line an agreement that gives us the right to bargain collectively for a union wage scale, and gives us better working
conditions.

ON STRIKE!

THE STRIKE CALL

For months I searched for work, from shop to shop, day in and day out. I walked through the dress market looking for one that needed my labor - but in vain. Worn out and fearful of those eager, searching eyes that met me every morning on the market, and as competitors we stared at one another.

Millions unemployed, breadlines, starvation, misery and evictions knocking at the door! Yet within the midst of the depression, a strike of dressmakers is called!

The German woman who sits next to me is about the only one that I had confidence in. She has a lovely motherly face with mild blue eyes that caress you every time they rest on one. They simply invite confidence. We were both new hands and very eager to keep the job.

"What a time to call a strike," she exclaimed.

"But, Helen, you know that conditions are unbearable and it's high time something is done to stop this misery!"

Helen bends her head lower. Instinctively I look up and meet the steel grey eyes of our boss. His look is like a dagger. It penetrates one's soul. All morning he has been like a lion in a cage. He has smelled danger in the air, and has kept his eyes on those he suspected to be troublemakers - as bosses love to call the ones that have courage to demand what is coming to them.

"Helen, please don't be frightened. He don't know that you belong to the union. He suspects only the Jewish girls!"

"But, it's not the lousy job I care for. It's only that I am so nervous. I simply can't wait till 10:00."

I look up. Only 8:30! What a long half hour! I look around me and take stock of those who will be likely to go down. On the other side of me is an old fat woman who hardly fits in the small hard chair. She would make a fine picture on a circus poster. I look at her out of one corner of an eye to see the expression on her face. It's blank. No hope! Opposite, two Italian girls who have probably never heard of a union. I try not to lose courage but my heart quivers when I think of what is in store for me.

The shop is unusually quiet this morning. It is before a storm, and we wait impatiently for the cloud to burst. At 9:30, a young girl with a red ribbon on her hair runs past me and whispers,

"Comrade, get ready for the struggle!"

The older worker looks up with contempt. "She must think it's a picnic! A fine time they pick to call a strike!"

"But what have we to lose?" I ask. "Nothing but our misery."

Will 10:00 never come? Fifteen minutes more! What's that! Like a black cloud the colored pressers are moving towards us. Fifty-three strong - the first ones to throw their work down! Just as a flame would spread through the shop, shaft after shaft is cleared. No power in the world can stop this moving cloud!

At that moment I felt like shouting. Beware! You who have pulled the rope too tight. You can never tell when it's liable to break!

THE 1909 STRIKE

I came to America in the year of 1909, being barely fifteen years of age. I had to go to work immediately, for I had to support, besides myself, the rest of my family in Russia. My sister had preceded me to this country by one year. She worked in a dress shop, and the Monday following my arrival I entered the shop where everything was ready to receive me.

The shop was small and dingy. There were three windows on either side of the building. We were forced to work the whole day by electric light. The front part of the shop was used as the office; on the other side stood the cutting tables, and the operators, finishers and pressors were crowded in the middle of the shop. This meant there was not a bit of sunshine nor air during ten hours at work daily. (This was in 1909, when we worked fifty-nine hours a week in the dress industry.) I do not care to describe the impression that the old sweat shop made on children of that age. It is too much to live through it again, if only for the brief period of writing it.

One fine day, a worker came over to me, and said "We will have a meeting." She put a piece of paper into my hands, which read as follows: "Workers of the dress industry, don't wait for the last call, come and join your union now."

Thus it happened that I entered a union hall for the first time in my life. The meeting was a huge success. The room was bitter cold, but no external heat was necessary. In a few minutes the room looked like a bee hive. The enthusiasm of the boys and girls, and their determination to win for themselves and their fellow workers a better living and a more respectable position in the industry, made the place the most lovable, warmest and most attractive spot in all New York City. For years after that I could not pass that hall without getting a thrill.

At that meeting, plans for the general strike of the ladies' waist and dressmaking industry were made. Being few in numbers, each and everyone of us was an important member of the organization. We practically had no experience at all. Even our leaders were for the most part the first time on a workers' battlefield. But in a very short period, our strike machinery was in full speed, and the winter of 1909 saw the most successful strike of the workers in the dress industry.

The final call came. We were to drop work at 10:00 in the morning. Everything was ready: committees, meeting halls, and speakers. Orders were given to everyone to leave his or her shop and bring as many workers as would respond to the first call. Everything was to be orderly as possible, so as not to frighten away the

unorganized workers, and to show them that there is nothing terrible
in a general walk out. The response was overwhelming. The first
couple of days saw the entire trade practically at a stand still.

Everyone in the shop I worked in stopped at 10:00 sharp,
I shall not forget that day in all my life. As said before, most
of the workers were concentrated in the middle of the shop, so that
we could have a fair view of every group. The operators, who have
always constituted the greatest number in the dress industry, were
the leaders of the strike, and everybody looked to this group of
workers for the signal to stop. The employers also knew where the
signal was bound to come from, and promptly planted the forelady to
keep an eye on who was going to be the first to drop work. While
she was watching the few active union girls, she was cheated of the
fun of being able to point out to the boss who gave the signal. At
the stroke of 10:00, the pressers put out their lights, and that
worked like a magnet. In a twinkling of an eye, all of the eighty
workers were on their feet and marched out of the shop in a most
beautiful and inspiring fighting mood, which lasted all throughout
the general strike.

WE GO OUT ON STRIKE

I got work, together with about twenty-five other girls, with a firm manufacturing children's dresses. My job was sewing on buttons, making buttonholes, trimming and packing dresses, as well as giving out work when Mr. K. was too busy to do it. For this I was receiving the magnificent sum of $13 a week and a promise of a raise "when business picks up."

Our shop consisted of a long narrow room with three windows on each end. The windows at one end were partitioned off for the office and cutting table, leaving the rest of the room with the light only from the three remaining windows. The rest of our conveniences consisted of a curtained corner with nails and hooks on the wall to hold our coats, a tin sink with a mouldy green faucet, and a toilet for which we had to stand in line during lunch hour.

Crowded together in this shop, the twenty-five of us lived like one big family. We did not go down for lunch often; it cost too much and it was not pleasant to climb four flights up and down when one got only three-quarters of an hour for lunch. So we worked, talked, ate and sang together for eight hours every day and for five and a half days every week.

L., a Spanish girl, managed to keep us laughing by making fun of everything, laughing heartily herself, her white teeth gleaming while speeding along with her work. The two M.'s were the ones who would start a beautiful Italian song in the afternoons when we were all getting tired. We would all join in, or else we would sing spirituals with J. and P. We loved to sing, but we didn't sing often, conditions were too wretched.

"I would sure quit this place if it wasn't that Bob and I are going to be married soon," J. would declare every second day or so.

"I am married, but I will sure have to take up some line to make my carfare and rent; after I pay for the eats there isn't anything left," would come from L.

"You go and tell that to the boss. Just yesterday as I was complaining about the price on style nine he told me 'You can take it or leave it; there are plenty others who would be glad to work.'"

"Don't let him be so snooty, this is positively the last week for me in this dump, look at this work. I won't even make enough to keep me in chewing gum!" exploded P., the flapper.

"What are you bellyaching for? Chewing gum isn't refined.
Mr. K. wants you to be a lady." This from L., of course.

"You are always talking of quitting as if that would help.
Quit this place and take a job in the sweat shop of Mr. K.
Don't you know that sweat shops are like the plague? They spread,
and you don't escape them by quitting."

"B. is preaching union again, girls," said one.

"It will take you five unions to get anything out of this
dump!" declared another.

"We don't need five unions. Smarter men than our boss have
had to pay more when the girls joined the union and struck," spoke
up M.

"Strike, and walk up and down the street like a fool, not
me! My boy friend wouldn't stand for that," and J. would wrinkle up
her pretty nose.

Our conversation would break up. The girls kept scanning
the want ad page every day. The bosses continued to set prices to
suit themselves.

It was a Thursday morning. The evening before we had received our pay. "I had a lousy pay for last week and it seems I'll
never make out any better this week either, not with this rotten
work. I am quitting!" exclaimed one girl, jumping up and throwing
her work aside. The girls all stopped work looking at her.

"Girls don't let's quit. Let's strike. Come on to the
union! Let's make this damn shop stop sweating everyone." I stand
up.

L. follows me. "I've had enough of this too," she says.
The girls all jumped up as they saw the boss coming on the run from
the other end of the shop.

"What's the matter? You don't like the work? We are cutting another lot of good work, you'll get it next, why -- er ---
you'll get it right away, it is ----"

"Oh yeah, we know your good work. We've had enough of it,
and we are on strike. Come on girls, we are going to the union."
My heart thumped fearfully as I said it. But the girls all followed
me, leaving our boss open mouthed.

MY FIRST STRIKE

When I first started to work in J. & J., it was not a union shop. I did not know what a union was. My boss was very friendly with me. She told me if I wanted her to be my friend I was not to make friends with anyone in the shop. The girls had told me to be very careful, because she was very fussy; she kept a girl about a month, then fired her and got someone else. I was afraid of losing my job and stuck by her and made no friends in the shop. Damn fool that I was, I was soon to know why.

A few weeks later there was a big argument in the shop. Mr. J. had gone over to the operators and told them he had to take 5 cents off every dress. The girls refused to take it. So he told them if they did not like it they could leave. After much argument and discussion they all accepted the cut. More and more dresses were coming out each week. Girls were working twice as hard as before.

A few weeks later, Mr. J. came around again and told them he had to take 5 cents more off, as dresses were selling cheaper. There was no argument this time; no one said a word. A week later he came around again and told the girls he was going to give them a nickel more on the dresses as he had gotten customers who would buy dresses for their usual price. There was much discussion among the girls that week of which I could learn nothing.

Next day my boss was out, there were three rings which meant for her to go in the office. I answered and said, "I'm sorry but Mrs. L. is out. Anything I can do for you?"

"No, we'll wait," was the answer. They were three men whom I had never seen before. She was out for quite a while; none of us knew where she was. About 4:30 she came in. I told her three men had come to see her. "Yes, yes," she said, "I know." Later I asked her where she had been. "I was tending to some business; we are getting more customers every day, so I think our prices will go up again." I said that was fine, because the girls were not the least bit satisfied with what they were getting. (Little did I realize why the prices were going up all of a sudden.)

Next morning when I went to work, I found the workers from my shop in front of the building. As I came towards them, the men approached me and told me not to go up to work as they were striking. Everywhere you went you could hear the word, strike, strike, strike! By asking a few questions I found that the girls had not even been making enough to live on.

We waited for about half an hour in front of the shop, then the organizer came and took us to the union. I should have said tried

to take us. What a time he had getting all of us to go. Some girls
belonged to the union before, and they said it was no good; others
said that if we joined, we would have to buy books and pay dues each
week, and when these books expired we would have to pay assessments
and get new books, and that the union would take a bribe from the
boss and we would get little or no increase in our wages. (This was
to be proved wrong.) Another girl who was very friendly with the
boss would not listen to any of the strikers. "No," she aid, "Mrs.
L. has been very good to me; she has been almost better than a mother
to me; I will not turn against her now!" Some girls told her that
that was just why she had been so good to her, so that when a strike
came she would not go out, but would try to convince the other girls
how wrong it was. I began to see why she did not want me to make
friends with anyone in the shop. When a strike came it would then
be hard for me to join the union.

The organizer began to talk, but they would not listen to
him. Then he said, "Well, come up to the union and sit there and
we'll discuss everything." After much persuading and nagging we all
went. There we found the general manager who talked to us and told
us of other strikes and how the girls acted and how they had won so
many times. Some girls got encouragement by this. Others came along
just to find out how we came out, but finally they became our most
active members.

We had day in and day out of picketing in front of the shop
without results. It seemed as though my boss got her work out just
the same. So we kept a closer watch on the shop. This was very hard
to do, because there were police everywhere. If you just stopped for
a minute, you were told to move on, and if you didn't do it, you were
shoved right into the patrol wagon. On one part of the street the
scabs in the shops above threw spools of thread at you. In addition
to this the police would come prancing up to the sidewalk on horseback and try to scare you away. But it seemed the more the police
threatened us, the stronger our force grew. More and more people
were joining us each day. People who knew nothing about our work,
used to come by and ask us how we were making out and wish us luck.
We sure needed it. A man in our shop was arrested for standing on
the corner with the paper under his arm. When he came back we asked
him if the judge sentenced him to the chair or life imprisonment.
"Neither," he answered, very sarcastically, "I was sentenced to hang
for the terrible crime I committed."

One morning about 11:00 our shop was called to the union
for a meeting. We were told that my boss had called up and told the
organizer to tell the girls if they wanted to come back to come now,
because after 3:00 he would take the 5 cent raise he had given them
back. There was much laughter in the union, everybody took it as a
joke. At noon we parted. The men went on the picket line and told
us girls to go and have lunch. When we came back they would go, so

we would have the shop covered all the time. Two days later my boss called the union again and told the girls if anyone wanted to come back they still had a chance. Everyone began to get uneasy; there seemed to be no results of our picketing and striking. It seemed as though the boss would not give in. The organizer told us to be patient; we would get what we wanted and more.

Next day the boss called up again and said he would give the operators 5 cents on every dress, but nothing to the finishers and pressers. This gave everybody courage. Girls said if he could give the operators 5 cents he could raise the finishers and pressers, too. The organizer called back and told him we did not agree; we wanted 10 cents for the operators and 5 cents for the finishers and pressers. This made him mad. That afternoon he called up again and said he would give 5 cents to the finishers and pressers but nothing more to the operators. There was much rejoicing in the union; now we knew our strike was almost won; we knew we would not come back till he gave the operators 5 cents more and cut down our hours. This made him furious, because we had asked for shorter hours in the beginning and he said, "no." As we did not say anything more, then, he thought we had accepted no.

He finally called up and told us he would give us shorter hours but no more increase in wages. We told him that if by 3:00 he had not given us the raise, we would ask for more. We were asking 50 and 60 cents on a dress as it was. To this he answered, "I'll think it over," in a very sarcastic manner.

My girl friend winked at me and nodded towards the door. I went out and she came directly after me. "Home to lunch as fast as you can," she said. "Why, what's the matter?" I asked. "Well," she said, "he's going to give the work out and we've got to watch where he brings it."

Well we watched from one corner of the street where we could see almost the entire block but could not be seen ourselves. We waited for about half an hour, when we saw the two "big shots" come out and look around everywhere. Luckily we were hidden or we would never have seen what we did see. They walked down one street where there were no shops to which they had ever given work and in the meantime kept turning back to see if they were followed. We kept following them on the other side, ducking in doorways, and finally we saw them enter a building. We wanted to follow them in but thought it unwise, so we hurried back to the union and told them about this. Everybody was very excited because we had found at last where they were giving their work out. Meantime it was quarter of 3:00. We decided that if the boss had not called by 3:00 we would ask for 2½ cents for the whole shop.

The organizers went to investigate this building while we waited for 3:00. About quarter of 4:00 the organizers came back and

118.

told us they had found the shop and had stopped it. We had not heard
from the boss yet so we called up and told the boss we wanted 2½ cents,
on every dress for everybody, and that if he did not tell us to come
back to work and give us what we asked for before 5:00, we would ask
for more. He did not answer us but told us he wanted to talk to the
organizer. He told the organizer to come right over that he would
fix everything up. Four organizers went down to the shop. At 4:30
we went on the picket line and stayed there till 6:00; then the men
came and relieved us, and told us to come back in the morning as we
would probably go to work.

Well I joined the union and got $2 a week increase per week;
the operators got 12½ cents per dress; the finishers got 7½ cents;
the cutters were on piece work and they were put on week work at $40
a week. We went back to work the next morning. Now our boss cannot
tell us, "If you don't like it, you can get out."

I am glad I joined the union because it gained so much, not
only for me and my shop, but it helped to organize many other shops
in our city. When girls of other shops knew what we gained, they
were more than willing to join.

SHIRT WORKERS STRIKE IN CINCINNATI

The shirt industry had not been organized until 1933, when a campaign was started in the east which brought into the Amalgamated Clothing Workers' Union about 30,000 new members. Efforts in Cincinnati were centered on two companies, each employing about 450 employees.

In 1933, several of the cutters in one of these companies, joined the union and began trying to organize the girls working in the stitching rooms. Their work was not rewarded until June, 1934, when three girls became so dissatisfied with conditions that they decided to go to the union meetings regardless of whether they would lose their jobs or not. They talked to some other girls, and about twenty of them went together.

The next day one of the first three girls was fired, and a special meeting was called. About eighty-five girls came to this meeting. Discontent ran high. Each one had her own special complaint. We decided to draw up a set of demands for union recognition. We knew we were up against stiff opposition, and did not expect to get what we were after without a fight. We took a vote, and the workers voted in favor of walking out if the demands were refused.

A committee was appointed to carry our demands to the boss, and the next morning at 8:30 we met and went down to the office. The vice-president got no farther than the first demand – the one for union recognition. His answer was a flat and final "No!" We hurried back upstairs ahead of the boss, and gave the prearranged signal for the strike. The shrill blasts of police whistles were enough to scare some of the workers out of the shop. Those who had not been taken into our confidence before were soon made aware of what was happening. We met outside the building and took account of our forces. About 150 came out, and we had only had eighty-five at the meeting! A good beginning!

We marched around the shop for about an hour, singing and shouting, but as few of us knew anything about carrying on a strike, our organizer told us to go to the union office where we would discuss plans. A few of us stayed on to direct any other workers who might decide to come out.

That was the beginning of our thirteen weeks' strike. It was a battle that started with friendly persuasion, but gradually took up more forceful weapons. The third day of the strike, a very militant group of strikers got together on a little plan of their own. Most of the girls employed in my shop came to town on street cars or busses, and walked a few squares through the heart of the city. The strikers stationed themselves at various corners along the route and waited with eggs – very "ripe" eggs! As the scabs came down the streets dressed in their fresh summer dresses, the war was on. The aim was not always perfect, but the majority of the "yellow" decorations found their proper resting places. The scabs were given a royal reception that morning, as they ran through the picket line before the shop. Jeers and howls of derision rang in their ears as they dashed past. At 9:30, the bosses decided to close the shop in order to protect their "loyal" employees from such indignities. Success number one for us! The shop was closed, and at no time during the strike was any attempt made to open it again.

But the fight had just begun. Long, hot days were ahead of us. Days when the thermometer quivered at 100-104 degrees. Days when rain poured down in sheets. But the picket line went on. Whether it rained or whether the sun shone, the steady line of pickets marched on, always singing lustily.

A special hall was rented for us, and we met there every morning for a short meeting and much inspired singing of labor songs. Organizers and active members were busy visiting and recruiting other workers into our ranks. Many had never even thought about a union for their protection, but after a convincing explanation they came over to the union side. Our numbers rose from 150 to 250.

Meetings with the company were arranged, but always ended without having made much progress. The employers were obstinate and not ready to talk reasonably to union representatives. They had run their business successfully for themselves; but what about their employees? Well, what did their employees have to complain about? Did they not always have work? Fair wages? What did the ignorant employees know about money matters? All they were interested in was "work." Did he not have any sympathy for his employees? Sympathy? No, he never did feel sorry for the people who worked for him; he gave them plenty of work, what more did they need?

Conferences began and ended much on the same note of antagonism and hatred against a union and any employee who dared raise his voice in protest against forty-two year old practices!

Fall orders started to come in, and the boss began to see his idle factory in the light of lost dollars to him. He finally agreed to recognize the union as representing the majority of his employees. A small increase in wages was included.

The union workers decided to accept the proferred contract as it made provision for the most essential demand: union recognition. Unionization was the first step, and each worker went back to work with hope and determination for the future, a future when every worker in the factory will be a member of the Amalgamated Clothing Workers' Union.

THE STRIKE AT MARION

The town of Marion, North Carolina, is very beautiful. It resembles a basin, the bottom being the city surrounded by beautiful mountains. It has a population of about 8000 people. About one mile from this pretty little town is the mill village, which is quite different in appearance.

Here we find unpaved streets of red mud and black cinders with no sidewalks. The houses are all exactly alike, and are in long rows up and down the mountain side. Some of them are painted very ugly colors while others have no paint at all. Lots of them are built on high stilts, so high you could easily park a car or house a cow under them. They are exactly like a box with four partitions dividing it into four and six rooms. These rooms are very small, and there are usually two open fire places to each house. The floors are very rough and splintered. There are no back porches but a high line of steps. In the back lot between every two houses you would find one toilet, to serve two families. These are open toilets a pit being only a few feet deep. They sometime over flow, then the toilet is moved to a new spot. About every four and six houses you will find an open pump on one side of the street. About four to six families from the opposite side of the street also get water from this pump which makes about eight or twelve families using water from the same well. Here the cows, chickens and children are all watered together.

On down the road is the mill itself, which is a large brick structure with a tall smoke stack from which the smoke pours daily only to settle on the dreary little homes of the workers. The company store is directly in front of the mill with a public highway between. The workers get paid sometimes in scrip, and this is redeemable in merchandise only at the company store. There are also two churches in the village, one Methodist and one Baptist, owned and partly controlled by the company.

On a hill overlooking the village is quite a different scene. Here is a nice little village apart from the workers, nice winding lanes, large shade trees, pretty flower gardens, nice paved streets and side walks, paved walks right up to the doors of large nicely painted houses. These houses have sun parlors, sleeping porches, heating systems, water systems and lights. These are the bossmen's homes, and this section is known as bossmen's row.

The mill was built some years ago and most of the workers are people who have come down from the mountains to work there. They manufactured cheap cotton goods.

The average wage was $10 and $11 per week in 1929. At this time the manager of the mill decided that twelve hours and twenty minutes a day with $10 and $11 a week wage was not enough work for the money. So he began to put on the stretch-out system, which meant that each worker should run twice the number of looms for the same amount of pay. The workers thought that with these long hours and such small pay the doubling of work was more than we could stand. Some of the workers thought we should organize, but we did not know just how to go about this.

At the same time there was a strike just over the hills from us in Tennessee. A few of the workers contributed $25 to pay carfare over there for two of our men to find out just how we should begin to organize. They were told that we should ask the A. F. of L. to send us an organizer. We immediately asked for and got one. In May 1929, the organizing began.

At first we had to meet in the woods, in old fields after dark, in vacant shacks or any place we could. As soon as the company heard of this, they began firing us. In a short time twenty-two had been fired. Some were told they were fired for joining the union; others were told nothing. But this did not stop our organizing. The people were so anxious to do something about their conditions that by the fourth of July out of 650 workers there were only thirty families who had not signed up with the union.

On the fourth of July, we for the first time appeared in public as an organization by staging a parade. How happy we all were. We were really trying now to do something about our conditions.

We elected a committee from among our workers to go before the manager with our grievances. At first he would not meet the committee. Then the president of the State Federation of Labor in Tennessee came over and talked to him. He then said he would at any time meet any committee from his workers with any questions they cared to discuss, and that none of them need be afraid they would lose their jobs.

Next day the committee went in again and he only wanted to know what it was all about. The next day a notice was put up in each department of the mill saying that the mill would stop at 5:30 and the mill president would talk to us on the mill lawn. This was something he had never done before. At 5:30 the mill stopped, and the workers all gathered to hear what he had to say. He had a platform erected and invited our organizer up to sit with him. He told us that the mill was built there and we had to come down to work here. He had built us nice homes to live in, given us good jobs and good wages, built good churches and a beautiful Y. M. C. A. for the workers (which cost from 10 to 25 cents to enter for anything there). He also mentioned the company store where we could get pay in scrip any time we wanted it and trade there. He said none of us had ever complained to him, and we had a very contented town until this outside agitator came in and stirred up trouble. He said he did not like the

things our organizer stood for, although he had no personal feelings
against him. He said he ought to get out and hoe flowers and lose
some weight, rather than stir up trouble among his workers. He said
we needed a boss, and when we could not mind the boss then we needed a master, and he would be the master. He asked us not to go to
any union meetings. He said he would take care of those who did not
follow the union, that the men could dig sewer lines and the women
could clean the bossmen's houses for half price to keep them going
through the fight.

As soon as he ended his speech the workers marched out into the road and followed the organizer to the speaking ground and the
president was left looking on.

The next day our committee went in again. They asked him
to give us ten hours a day at the present wage scale, to improve
sanitary conditions, to reinstate the ones he had fired for joining
the union, and to recognize the union.

He said he would not but he dared them to strike by offering them $5 each to pull the strike. After we heard the report, ex-
citement ran high.

In a few days our committee went in for the third time.
This time he said no, but he would give each of them $50 to pull a
strike.

In the meantime the night hands had all gathered around the
store, and when the committee came out they did not have to tell us
he had refused, they knew by their looks. In less than five minutes,
everything in the mill had stopped and the workers were again on the
lawn.

Next morning before 6:00, we formed a picket line around the
mill. No one came to work; and for nine weeks we kept up our picketing and not a wheel turned.

One day "the boss" wanted some cotton unloaded. We insisted
that he take union men in to help him, but he wanted scabs. As he
went through, the heavy gate flew back and hit him. He called for
his deputies and fourteen of our boys were arrested. He was not hurt
he received only a bump from the gate.

About one-half mile from East Marion there are two mills
known as Clinchfield. These mills employed about 1000 workers. They
also began to put on the stretch-out, and the workers began to organize. They were fired wholesale. One hundred and fifty were fired in
one day. Then the mills closed down, and the workers were told that
when they were needed again they would be notified. For some time the
mills remained closed, and the workers declared it was a lockout. The
day after the lockout was declared, they decided to open it up. Picket

lines were formed all around the mills. The Governor sent his representative in, and told the organizer if he did not make the people move and open the gates he would call the soldiers. Of course it was up to the workers and not the organizer to decide what to do. We stood firm, and did not open the gate. The soldiers were called but did not come into the village for two weeks. Next day we did let the gates be opened and a few went to work.

This, of course, meant more people had to be fed. Funds seemed to come in slowly. The U. T. W. had just conducted a strike in Tennessee and did not have funds to take over another strike. The Emergency Committee, Civil Liberties Union and Brookwood Labor College helped with funds. Even though we had to go two and three days without enough food and though the food was the cheapest and roughest kind and very scarce, with twelve pounds of flour and a small piece of white meat which we called "salty pork," we continued our fight. We were content with what we got and were determined to stick. You would often hear remarks on the picket line such as, "I'll picket and eat salty pork till I sweat lard before I give up." Sometimes we would build a large fire and get a wash pot, and some farmer would give us roasting bars, and we would cook at night on the picket lines and eat corn from the cob. We would gather around the fire singing songs and dancing by the string music.

During all this time we had tried to get a settlement with the boss but could not.

A house which rented for 80 cents per week was raised to $4.50 per week. Eviction papers were served. An injunction was issued, which we carried to Court and successfully defeated.

One day a family was being evicted and the strikers only stood by and looked on. It was almost too much to take so calmly. After the officers of the law had carried out the furniture, some of the strikers carried it back and put it in place. No one was hurt and we had no violence. In less than an hour, forty-eight of our men were arrested and one little girl. People who were not on the ground were arrested, some who were miles away. The little girl, who weighed about 110 pounds, was arrested for assaulting the sheriff who weighed over 250 pounds. The men were charged with inciting a riot, insurrection and rebellion against the state.

Then the soldiers came into the village and were also sent to East Marion. They opened the mills, and all who wished to and were not in the union went to work. They tore down our little picket shacks and stretched nice new tents for themselves. The people were not allowed to go to the post office. We had to walk the streets one by one; and every car, man and woman who went down the road was searched and even pocket knives taken. They treated us terribly.

Finally an agreement was reached for both mills. Clinchfield was going to stop night work and take back enough workers to complete the day shift. This left about 500 Clinchfield workers completely out, with no hopes of work there. They planned to work fifty-five hours a week at the present wage scale. East Marion was to work fifty-five hours, install a water system in the village with no discrimination against union members. At the end of six weeks we were to let **"the boss"** know if we would rather work sixty hours or fifty-five hours.

We had never been able to have a closed meeting, for we had no place to meet. That night we were allowed to go to the school house to discuss the settlement. We were told that all of us could go back to work except fourteen families. We did not have a written agreement, only a statement by a representative of the Governor, reported to us by one of our organizers. However, he did not tell us to accept it or not to accept it. We knew that the company, the law, the public, the churches, and the soldiers were all there and were against us. A vote was taken, the agreement was accepted although a large number of us did not approve and did not vote. Next day when we went to get out passes to go to work we found that not fourteen families were left over but 150 families were unable to go to work.

By this time the relief was very, very scarce and we knew that something would have to be done. For a period of three weeks we tried to get a conference with the mill president, but he had gone to Baltimore and did not come back for some time. We wanted him to know that the agreement had been broken so we wired him. He said he would be in in a few days. When he did come he refused to meet the committee again.

On the first of October, the workers who had gone back to work said we had all fought together for the same thing and they would not leave us. They wanted to come out and stay with us until we all got back together. The superintendent learned that something was coming off, so he called the sheriff to come down at 11:00 and bring his deputies. All night there was a growing excitement and tense feeling in the mill. A boss pointed his gun at one worker and dared him to shut off the power machine. Finally the boy did shut off the power and the workers walked out for the second time, in the face of starvation. As daylight came the pickets assembled in the road and the sheriff and his fourteen deputies were in and around the mill gate. Most of the deputies were workers in the mills who were opposed to the union. As the whistle sounded, the superintendent ordered the people to move out of the road and let the scabs in; but the poor strikers stood firm. The sheriff then threw tear gas into the crowd. The people began to run and the sheriff and his force began to fire at their backs. Forty or fifty shots were fired and played in the dust like drops of rain. The people were darting everywhere for protection.

When the firing stopped the road was full of dead, dying and wounded just like bees or flies crawling - some trying to get up, some dead, and some groaning and moaning and struggling for life. Blood ran in streams from their poor frail bodies. An old man, past sixty

years, who was a paralytic, was blinded by the gas and began to grapple
in the dark for something to hold to. While grasping he touched the
sheriff, who turned on him held him by the shoulder and shot him down
then placed handcuffs on him. He was later carried to the hospital,
put on the operating table and died with handcuffs still on him.

A few cars came up to pick up the wounded and carry them to
the hospital. Some of the wounded were so anxious to get there they
merely hung on the backs of cars, and when they arrived at the hospital
were unconscious. The hospital had been built about two years before
and the money had been collected in the mills from the workers to help
build it. We were told that it would be a community hospital and if
we needed to go there it would cost us nothing. When the poor strikers
were piled on the floor they were left to scramble in the blood from
their wounds and suffer a living death until messages could be sent to
New York and back assuring the hospital that they would get money for
the treatment of the strikers. When they were picked up four of them
were dead and twenty-eight wounded.

Next day we had a funeral for the dead. Four grey caskets
were placed in a row on rough frames made by the strikers. The
caskets were joined together with a white and yellow ribbon which had
U. T. W. of A. on each ribbon. The platform was beautifully decorated
with flowers tied with paper bows of blue and white. The ground underneath the caskets was a carpet of flowers. The mill president sent
word down that he had some very nice flowers; if we wanted any he would
have them sent down. But what did flowers from his garden mean now to
his dead workers. We did not take any. There was not a local minister
who would conduct the funeral service for those men - they had all
taken sides against us. Rev. James Myers of the Federal Council of
Churches conducted the services. Thousands of people attended the
funeral. After the services, the strikers marched two abreast behind
the hearses carrying flowers. We went right down by the mill and over
the spot where they had been killed on to the cemetery.

In the meantime, a load of cinders had been dumped by the
company on the road covered with blood. The mill ran full speed that
day. The president said that the shooters were damned good marksmen -
forty or fifty shots fired and thirty accounted for. If he every organized an army he would give them a job.

While these four were being buried, another died and then
another, which made six killed. The soldiers were called again, not
to protect the poor workers who were fired on. They were placed around
the mill and the sheriff's home.

We realized that something must be done about the people out
of work. So we sent a committee to the judge and told him the agreement had been broken. He said he could not remember anything that was
said in the conference. Then the Committee went to the State Governor
himself. They asked him to investigate and find out whether or not

the agreement had been broken, the wages and hours in the mill, the character of the deputies, and the financial standing of the mill. He told them he had no power to do this and he did not investigate. The president carried the Governor a nice bunch of flowers and asked him to keep the soldiers in Marion a while longer although the strikers had protested. So the soldiers stayed.

In the meantime, the sheriff, his deputies and the bosses were arrested on charges of murder. They were given a hearing and all were freed but two bosses, the sheriff and a few deputies who were held on a second degree murder charge. They were bonded out by the president. In December they were tried, and all were acquitted. Our organizer and strikers were not allowed to move their trials to another county but had to be tried in McDowell county. They were found guilty of inciting a riot. The organizer was fined $1,000 and costs, while the boys were sent to serve six months on the county chain gang.

We then reorganized our relief work. The Federal Council of Churches came in and took the situation over for three months and they did a very good job. We got very fair food and some medical attention. A lot of clothing was sent in and given out. Long lines of people would stand in the snow for a whole day at a time waiting for relief. Some hungry and some with not enough clothes to keep themselves warm. The East Marion Baptist Church issued fifteen letters of dismissal, and one man was excluded from the church for the simple reason that he had joined the union.

The opening of school was delayed two weeks, and when it did open no child was allowed to speak of the strike, and if a lesson on labor questions came up it was omitted. Magazines of any kind carried to school by the children were carefully looked over before the child could keep them.

Evictions from company houses came very rapidly. On New Year's day, we saw several families thrown in the street in the snow. An old man who was sick in bed was carried to the road in a chair. The workers built a fire to keep him warm. Some women had their food on cooking and this was put in the street too. Some of them simply set up their oil stoves in the road and cooked right on. These workers had no place to go. Most of the land was owned by the company. They were doubled up in small shacks, dugouts and basements — anywhere they could get to stay.

One night a little boy was playing on a hillside. It was almost dark when a scab came out of his house and fired a shot gun. An hour later a man came down the road and found the little fellow behind some bushes struggling. He had forty-two shots in his little body. He struggled for ten months and then died. Two women had seen the gun fired, knew the man who did it and yet the sheriff said he had no clues and no evidence to arrest anyone.

All the time the mill was filling up with workers from the
outside and the strikers were left to starve. All forms of relief
stopped, a lot of sickness had developed and the people were in a
terrible condition. We had tried so hard to find work but owing to
the blacklist we could not find any.

A small group of women began to <u>try</u> to make hooked rugs.
We knew nothing about it. We had no money, no material and it looked as though we would have to give it up. We kept on trying and
finally sold a few. A dollar meant a lot to us when we did not have
anything. Some are still making rugs, but as fast as we can find
work we move out of Marion.

Our strike is over, each grey little house in the village
has a new room at the back which is the new bath room. The workers
in the mill now have a ten hour work day, but we have no organization
of any kind.

There are still some families there who need help, the
greatest suffering does not come while the fight is hotest, but
after a strike is lost when so many are left to do the best they
can. Although we sacrificed and suffered more than we can tell,
there still runs deep in us a strong desire to fight it out yet,
and accomplish something worth while. The cost of life and blood
was too great for us to lose our fight.

THE DANVILLE STRIKE

Danville is a small town with a population of 40,000 in northern Virginia. The Dan River and the Riverside Cotton Mills, located here, are the largest and oldest mills in the South, having been in operation for forty-six years. They are owned and run by natives of Virginia, and produce all kinds of fancy ginghams, broadcloths, shirtings, handkerchiefs, sheeting and bedspreads.

Schoolfield is the mill village of the company on the outskirts of Danville. Most of the company houses in the village are box houses built on stilts, some high enough to park cars beneath. A small grate which holds about a half gallon of coal is the only means of heating the rooms of the houses. Toilets are built in the back lots. The streets are cinder roads, and most of them have paved sidewalks. One street has very nice houses on it, but the rent is so high that only "second hands" can afford to live there. The mills have beautiful lawns, flower beds and shade trees around them.

The conditions in the mills were almost unbearable. The workers were not allowed to speak to each other during working hours. The girls were timed when they went to the lavatories. The lunch period was twenty-five minutes. Work started at 6:55 in the morning and stopped at 5:30, with a fifty-five hour week. If we were not inside the gate at 6:50, we lost a day's work, for the gates were locked after that time.

When we enter the mills in the morning a hot wave of steam meets us and continues all day. Not all departments allow the windows to be opened. Humidifiers keep the air damp.

Wages in the mill were low. We made $6, $8, $9, $11 and $14 a week for fifty-five hours. On top of all this, three years ago the company introduced the stretch-out system. Before this the girls in the weave room ran from twelve to eighteen looms and made from $25 to $27 per week. After it was introduced, they ran from twelve to sixty-four looms, making from $17 to $18 per week. If the girls did not get out a certain production each day, the boss threatened to fire them. It was impossible for the workers to get a production off that many looms for they could not keep them running. If they happened to make a little bad place in the cloth, the boss had them up at the cloth table to look at it, and docked them for the whole cut, so that they got nothing for weaving it. This stretch-out system applied to departments all over the plant. The workers did more and got less pay for doing it.

On the first of January, 1930, the president of the mills, posted a notice saying that the employees would receive a 10 per cent wage cut, effective February 3, 1930. At this time, the loom-fixers had a union among themselves which they had formed eleven years before. The company also had a company union in the mills known as "Industrial Democracy," which had been formed eleven years before. This company union was set up with a House of Representatives for the workers, a Senate for the overseers, a cabinet for the company officials and with the veto power in the hands of the president of the mills. We were supposed to send in our grievances through the House and in this way protect the wage cut. But the president told us he was going to cut wages regardless of what the people thought, and if any one did not like it, he could go elsewhere and God bless him. He also discharged two of the representatives for protesting against the wage cut.

With this unbearable stretch-out system and the wage cut, we had more than we could stand. So we sent a committee of loomfixers to Richmond, Virginia, to see if Mr. Green, who is the president of the American Federation of Labor, would send an organizer into Danville. He sent two.

We held our first meeting on January 9, 1930, with about 1500 workers present, and we wrote up about 1000 applications after the meeting. From this, our organization kept growing, and the company started firing our members for their union activities. By the first of April, they had discharged 250 union members. We sent a committee to see the president and ask him if these people could not be put back to work. He said, no, that none of these people would ever work for him again.

The company officials said we did not have over 300 members in the union, so we decided to show them. On April 5, 1930, we had a protest parade of 4,000 workers. We marched from the union office to Ballou Park, a distance of about four miles. We went right through the center of the town up Maine Street. Two policemen led the parade, on white horses, the band was next to them and then came the workers. You could not hear a sound except the patter of feet. When we arrived at the Park we had speaking and sold cold drinks to cover the expense of the parade.

Then from June 9 to June 14 we held a Chautauqua in the fair grounds. We had another nice week with no violence. President Green spoke to us on Saturday night, June 14.

On July 4, we had a picnic in the Park with speakers and the band, and everything went off nicely. On August 1, the company shut down two plants throwing 1500 of our members out of work. By the first of September, they started these plants up again by going out of town to get people to put on our jobs, and left us all on the street. We knew if this continued we would lose our organization, and all of our members who were still at work said they would not stand for it. They all wanted to strike, but our leaders advised us not to because of the depression all over the country. They knew it was the wrong time to call a strike. But the people were not satisfied; so when the United

Textile Workers had a convention in New York on the first of September, the union endorsed our strike. The strike vote was taken on September 17 and 18, 1930. When the votes were counted, they were 95 per cent for the strike. On Sunday, September 29, 1930, the strike was called. Four thousand strikers and their families made 15,000 people to feed.

On Monday morning we formed our picket lines around the gates, but the gates did not open. Scabs walked around the streets and looked at the pickets. We continued to picket without any violence, but an injunction was served on us the first day, and they continued to serve injunctions on us all the time we were on strike.

The strikers had to line up to get food, and sometimes we would stand in line all day, and then have to go home at night without any thing as the commissary was empty so much of the time. We only got fat meat, beans, potatoes and flour, and sometimes there was nothing for several days at a time. But we stayed right on the picket line without a kick even when we were hungry and cold. Hardly any of the men had overcoats and all of them were very thinly clad. Some had holes through the bottom of their shoes but they did not grumble even though picketing in deep snow. Some of the families had no food in their houses and nothing to make a fire with. Their children got sick and they could not even get a doctor. The children cried for something to eat and there was no way of getting it. It was terrible to see just what these people did go through with.

About 300 children went barefoot there all winter. People were evicted from their homes and set right out in deep snow with nowhere to go and nothing to eat and their children crying from cold and hunger. All the children were underweight because they could not get enough to eat. The men went out to cut wood to make heat for their families.

In November, the Governor sent in eight companies of troops, and they would not let the strikers picket. The soldiers went across the North Carolina line and escorted people over to take the strikers' jobs in the mill. The day these troops were sent into Danville, the picketers picked up the car of the president of the mill, turned it around and told him to go back home. They also turned some of the scabs' cars around and sent them back home, but there was no violence. They simply picked the cars up and turned them around. That was not the cause of the soldiers coming in, however, for they were already on their way to Danville before that happened.

That same morning the Chief of Police threw a tear gas bomb into the crowd of strikers to scatter them. But he would not let any of his men shoot. The Chief was very friendly to the strikers up until that time, but the newspapers were nasty to us all the time. A good many of the strikers were arrested and charged with dynamiting and other things, but none of them were convicted since they could

not prove anything on them. We had a wonderful lawyer, Mr. Williams.
He gave his services to the strikers free. Governor Pollard came to
Danville and tried to get a settlement but he was told by the mill
president to go home and mind his own business. Every means had been
tried to get a settlement, but to no avail. The relief was out and
there was sickness and terrible distress in the homes. The Red Cross
said it would come into Danville when the strike was settled, but it
would not come in while the strike was on. Mr. Morgan, the president
of a coal company, acted as a negotiator between the union and the
company. Mr. Morgan's statement was that the strike was called off
and the people believed they would get their jobs back and still hold
their union cards. When they went to get their jobs, they were told
that they were not needed in the mills.

      With so much sickness, the commissary empty, no money com-
ing in to buy food and people starving and freezing, the leaders
thought probably it was best to call the strike off. They took the
vote and it was called off January 29, 1931, exactly four months
from the day it was called.

      About 1500 people got their jobs back out of the 4,000
strikers. A good many of these people have left Danville, but there
is a lot of suffering yet. The Red Cross refuses to help any more.
The people of Danville put up a good fight and showed plenty of
courage all the time, but they lost their strike because of the depression all over the country. They could not raise enough money
to feed the people, although they did all they could under the economic conditions. The United Textile Workers of America sent in between $38,000 and $39,000. The money, clothes, food, and everything
that was spent in Danville for the strikers amounted in all to about
$150,000.

      Although we lost our strike in Danville, we did gain some-
thing. The organization of the union and the strike that took place
educated the people to what an organization means not only in Danville but all through the South. Despite the fact that we lost the
strike, we are still trying to carry on organization work in Danville.
Organization is the only salvation for the workers.

THE NEW HAVEN NECKWEAR STRIKE

New Haven was the town to which the New York neckwear industry moved when it tried to get out of paying union rates, working union
hours and having all work done on the inside of the shop. From 1927
on, several New York plants moved to New Haven or started contract shops
there. The first plant was picketed by strikers from the New York Neckwear Makers' Union, and New Haven girls soon talking to the pickets
were arrested. These plants paid relatively high wages for girls' work
in New Haven, although the hours were long. Much of the work was also
given out as home work.

The third plant to move from New York was S.'s, considered
one of the largest shops there. It was established in New Haven in
August, 1930, and employed 350 workers. Before the opening of the
factory, we were promised raises in the wage scale, but we did not
get them. We started work immediately after the factory was settled,
and worked steadily. Hours were from 7:30 A.M. to 5:30 P.M. Then
came the Christmas rush orders. With only a few experienced workers
from former neckwear plants and a large amount of new help who were
not very efficient, our hours were prolonged. Workers resented this,
but felt that they were indebted to the employer because he had been
so good to them and had given them parties.

During the months of August to December, organizers from the
United Neckwear Makers' Union of New York started an organizing campaign. They had a great many difficulties in organizing people. The
fact that most of the workers were of Italian extraction, and were
mere children dominated by their families with no say of their own,
made organizing a hard task. People in New Haven were ignorant of
the importance of a union and would not listen to the organizers.
After a great deal of hard work a few small groups were organized.

The experienced workers in S.'s averaged from $25 to $30
with overtime. In the month of October, prices were cut 5 per cent.
From that time on, a few workers realized the importance of a union
and became active in the union groups. But most of the workers felt
obliged to the employer for his kindness, and let matters remain as
they were. The employer was informed of the organizers visiting his
workers, called a meeting of the workers and threatened to discharge
any person affiliated with the union. This was quite a blow and dis-
couraging to the union officials, because many workers dropped out
of union meetings for fear of losing their jobs. The employer also
compelled the workers to sign a paper ordering the arrest of any organizer visiting unwanted the homes of the workers. During the busy
months in this plant, inexperienced girls from fourteen to sixteen
years of age worked eleven hours a day and Sunday morning, receiving
only $8 weekly. They were promised pay for overtime but did not get
it. The employer did not actually compel workers to work overtime,

but those who did not come in received the bad work because all good work was given to girls who worked overtime and on Sundays.

A man who has scabbed the job from New York was a foreman in S.'s. He was working his way in to become shop manager. Sam and S. were very good friends in New York and New Haven. Rudy, the shop manager, was about to lose his job so he communicated with the union organizers. He voluntarily offered to help pull off the strike if afterward his job as manager would be permanent. This he was assured of because with the difficulties organizers found in organizing a few, it was going to be just as hard a struggle to organize the remainder, who formed the bulk of the workers. He asked the organizers to send a couple of girls to help pull the strike which was to take place February 20.

In the latter part of January, however, the employer gave the girls two cuts, and on February 5, 1931, another cut. This made the workers furious and more determined than ever to do something about it. Before doing anything rash, four girls were picked from each operation for a conference with the employer who was in town this day. One group after another consulted the employer as to the outrageous wage cuts they got all in one month. The girls threatened to do something if he did not raise the wages. He said he would give them his answer the next morning as to whether he would raise the wages or not. The next morning the shop was in a turmoil. Every one was waiting for the boss's answer. He did not call so the girls telephoned him and he was still undecided. This broke down the old feeling of loyalty of the workers and being a psychological moment, they went on strike. The majority of the workers, unaware of the fact that the union officials were waiting for them, joined them when they were told to go to a hall for a meeting. The strike was 100 per cent walkout and all workers attended this first meeting. Rudy's help in pulling the strike was not yet revealed to the workers. After the strike meeting, workers agreed to stick together and continue their fight for demands. The next day, which was Saturday, February 6, another meeting was held which was also 100 per cent in membership. But on Sunday, February 7, strikers received telegrams asking them to show their loyalty to Rudy and attend a meeting at the factory at 3:30. After receiving this telegram, the strikers did not know what to do. The organizers heard of this and tried their best to visit the homes of as many strikers as possible and tell them not to go to this meeting but to theirs. Many went to Rudy's meeting before the organizers reached them. Others, who were children dominated by their parents, were forced to go. About 200 attended this meeting, and on Monday morning one hundred returned to work. It was on this day that Rudy's help to pull the strike was revealed and also his double-crossing the union.

We started picketing in masses trying to dissuade workers from going in to work. During the next week, fifty of the hundred workers came out, the remaining fifty being instructors and foreladies. We visited their homes at night trying to persuade them to come out on strike with us, but they ignored us and sometimes put us out of their homes. The employer brought Rudy over and caused him to double-cross the union. Rudy, because of his magnetic personality, thought that he would get all the workers back. But the strikers were determined more than ever to fight against him.

Our mass picketing was ended when an injunction was issued limiting the number of pickets. We did not get much publicity, only when strikers were arrested. We picketed peacefully and were told it was an orderly picket line. Daily meetings were held at Fraternal Hall with speakers from all over the country. Strike benefits of $10 were paid to all strikers, who were satisfied because it was a larger amount than they made in the mill after the wage cuts. After one month on strike, the mill was filled with strikebreakers.

Mr. S., the employer, was about to settle, but was told to hold out a little longer by the Chamber of Commerce. They knew that if this strike were won, the shirt factories, pants factories, etc., would all follow in striking. The conditions in those factories were as bad as ours and in some instances worse. The Manufacturers' Association backed S. financially. During the strike his orders were boycotted and he had very little work for the strikebreakers.

Students of Yale University were very interested in our strike and picketed with us. They also attended meetings. The wife of the president of the Chamber of Commerce was in sympathy with us and picketed with us. A check of $10,000 was endorsed by the Executive Committee of the New York Local and a promise made to finance the strike till the end. After four months, our strike benefit was reduced to $7. Each neckwear maker of the New York Local gave 10 per cent of his pay in the busy season to help pay strikers, and after three months the slow season brought it down to 7 per cent of their wages.

A conference was brought about with the employer and the strikers which resulted in no agreement nor settlement. A proposition was made by the employer saying he would take back seventy-five girls that week and 100 during or in the busy season in September. The strikers rejected this proposition.

The United Neckwear Makers' Union is affiliated with the A.F. of L. Before the neckwear industry became organized, conditions in the mills were terrible and the boys and girls in their teens worked from sunrise to late hours of the evening. The quickest and most experienced worker earned $5 or $6 a week. Neckwear workers first became organized in 1903. During its first twenty years the union was very strong; only four strikes prevailed during those years, all of which were successful. The United Neckwear Makers' Union is not an international union, but since 1927, when the manufacturers left New York to escape the union, the union has extended its activities elsewhere. There are 2,200 members in this union altogether.

THE 1931 HOSIERY STRIKE IN PHILADELPHIA

On the morning of January 13, 1931 mother called me to tell me there was trouble in the L. Mill. Dad's foreman had to pass this shop on his way to work, and he had seen pickets walking up and down the pavement. This was a surprise to me, as everything had been quiet on Tuesday when I left the shop. I called my brother, who also worked in the shop, and we decided to go to the union and find out what the trouble was.

When we got to the Union Hall, we waited for one of the officers to arrive. C., the first vice-president of our local, was the first to come. I asked him, "What is the trouble at the L. shop? I hear they are on strike. Is this true or not? I work there, and don't want to be a scab."

C. replied, "Yes, it is true there is a strike. It was called for various reasons."

He then told me the reasons. Mr. B., the owner, had bought a lot of very bad silk at a cheap price. When the stockings were finished and shipped to a New York department store, the store would not accept them, but returned them stating they were not perfect stockings. In our shop, the worker had to pay for all his or her bad work if the work was allowed to go through to the finishing department. So, the next thing for our beloved boss to do was to return the stockings to the knitters with a slip of what they owed the firm. These men received from one to sixty-nine pairs of hosiery for which they had to pay 75 cents a pair.

Four men, who were night workers and union members, did not feel this was fair. They walked out of the shop and went to the union. There being a law against a walk out, they were sent back to the shop. When they arrived at the shop, they were informed they were fired. Other men were put on these jobs with the permission of the union, as these men were also union members, to help prepare for the strike.

After being given this information, I was instructed to go into the shop and finish my work, and to try to bring as many out with me as possible. When I arrived in the shop, the boss was running around like a mad man, running his hands through the seven or eight hairs he had, pacing up and down the room, first howling at one then the other at the top of his voice. Some of the girls and fellows stopped work, and would not start up again until they found out what it was all about, for we had quite a few union girls and fellows working in this shop. I told them I had been to the union, and that C. had said, "Work until 2:00 and bring the night shift along with you to Union Hall for a meeting."

Mr. B. heard this, and said, "You're crazy to listen to that bunch down there." He had once been a very strong union member himself, and one of the "bunch."

It was quite some time before the workers would even consider returning to their jobs. Mr. B. even raised the price, which he had reduced several weeks before, on this style of work to try to get the girls and fellows to work, but they refused to be bought. We did work until 2:00, and then with some of the night workers we had, we had our first strike meeting of the shop. There were about twenty who attended, as the shop was not working full.

On arriving at the hall, we were met by the organizing committee. I was handed a book and a pencil, and made secretary of the shop strike committee. We were then told how to picket the shop, and how to arrange the picket list. I took down all the names of those present and arranged them in groups of fours to be assigned different shifts. The first shift went on at 6 A. M. to 9 A. M.; the second, from 9 A. M. to 12 noon; the next, from 12 noon to 3 P. M.; and the last from 3 P. M. to 6 P. M. Thus the shop was covered at all times.

The boss then called in those who were not working to take the jobs of those who had struck. The pickets were on the job at 6 A. M. the next morning to tell anyone who came to work that there was a strike. Some of the former employees went in, while others joined the strikers. The boss said to me, "You have no reason to be on the picket line or on strike either, as the trouble does not concern you. It is not the chiffon workers who have had the trouble." I said, "When my union calls a strike on a shop in which I am working, regardless of whether it is my work or not, it is my duty to come out." He then walked away. It is interesting to know that the chiffon workers gave up good jobs and made the sacrifice, in spite of the fact they were not involved, to join their fellow workers in time of trouble. The chiffon workers were being paid the union scale of pay, and had been working steadily up until this time.

This shop was located in a very isolated part of the city. There were few stores or places where we could go to get a cup of hot coffee, or get warm on a cold morning. Next to the mill was a store and restaurant where we went to get coffee. The scabs and police also went there. One day, Jim, the storekeeper, said, "You can no longer come into the store. Mr. B. told me if I let you come he would not allow the scabs or cops to come in; and when the strike is over I will have to move, as there will be no business for me as the union will win the strike." The cops would go into this store and order chicken dinners, pie, cake, and buy as many cigars and cigarettes as they wanted. The storekeeper gave the bill to Mr. B. Sometimes these bills ran up to $100 a week. This was done to get the cops to side with the boss and the scabs.

The cops were not very friendly to the pickets. One sergeant was quite a bully. If a girl or fellow stopped or said something to anyone approaching the shop he would say, "Move on and stop your talking or I will run you in." He also hit one of our fellows. We had a warrant sworn out for him and had him removed from the shop. The next sergeant was quite different. He sometimes gave the pickets a smile instead of a black look. He acted as if it were a duty. He did not like to have to be planted in front of a struck shop. He would not allow the scabs to holler at the pickets or pass remarks. This also applied to the strikers. There was very little trouble on the picket line. If a picket would get fresh he would come to me and say, "If so and so passes remarks or causes disturbance, I will have to arrest him but.I am telling you first." This sergeant thought I had a great deal of influence over the strikers; he had also been told by the boss I was the real leader. Without me he could win as I kept the fight up in the rest of the group. I was also blamed for everything that happened. One day, we had volunteer pickets on the line. Mr. B. came out of the shop in his shirt sleeves.and, pointing to the volunteer pickets, said, "They have no right to picket here as they never worked here." First the cop ordered the volunteers off the line and the pickets protested, but in the end they went for an automobile ride to the station house. When the case came up, the magistrate told the cop he had no right to arrest a peaceful picket. We were then allowed to have volunteer pickets. This made Mr. B. very angry.

I was out on strike not quite one month when the union called a general strike on all non-union shops in the city for the purpose of organizing and trying to stabilize the trade. This would mean all manufacturers would pay the same wage and therefore sell similar grades of hosiery for about one price, thus doing away with competition. In the previous two and a half years, the union shops in the competitive area had very little work, while non-union shops were working sixteen to eighteen, and twenty-four hours a day. Up to this time there had been eleven shops out on strike for one reason or another.

On February 16, 1931, the general strike was called. At around 10:30 A. M., the strikers started to drift into our Union Hall. They came by machine, trolley, foot -- all eager to fight for better conditions and to help save the trade. Some of these shops came out 100 per cent, while from others there were only a few who had the courage to walk out. As these people arrived, they were instructed to select a chairman and secretary to represent the shop where they worked. Most of those girls and fellows had never been in a strike, nor had they belonged to a union, but all were eager to learn and very anxious to join. For all they had steady work, the boss was continually cutting pay and making them work longer hours. In some of these shops, a worker worked seven days a week; and if there was any defect in the stocking he made, he had to pay for it.

At 2:30 that afternoon we had our first general strike meeting. When the roll of shops was called, forty-three answered with a representation of about 4,000 workers. Four suburban shops were also represented. Instructions were given about picketing the shop. Each secretary assigned the workers into groups of four or more, according to the size of the shop, in shifts of two or three hour periods. These shifts started at 6 A. M. and continued until 6 P. M.

The strikers were sincere, and in few cases did they ask what the union was going to give them for giving up their jobs. These strikers were girls and fellows from sixteen years old and up. There were also married men with families, but that made no difference -- they were out to fight and help save a trade so they might make a decent living wage.

Every afternoon we held strike meetings where the shop reports were read and the progress of the strike was told. We had very interesting speakers in the labor movement come and tell of the different difficulties of other unions and to encourage us to fight on.

After these meetings which lasted up until about 4:30 P. M., we would all go to one shop in a mass picket, to make an impression on the scabs -- if this was at all possible. In most cases we were greeted by twenty or thirty cops, who somehow found out where we were going. In many cases we could not get within a block of the shop. If we tried, we were beaten with clubs or shoved.

It was not unusual for three or four hundred to be arrested a week. The director had issued a statement that he would break up the strike if he had to arrest all the pickets and hold them under bail and bankrupt the union, which he sure did try to do. We were beaten over the head and back with clubs. One sergeant gave orders to "crack the skulls of the damn pickets."

We often wondered how the cops would find out so quickly where the mass picket was going. One day one of the fellows saw another go out of the hall just after the shop was announced. The next day he was followed to a candy store where he telephoned. After he came out, one of the boys went in and asked the lady if she knew the number called. She said, "Yes," and gave the number. We traced it, and found it belonged to a detective agency where they had each shop numbered. On getting the call, they called the nearest station house to the mill. In that way the cops would arrive either before us or shortly after. The next day a group of six strong-armed fellows took this boy and threw him out of the hall, and he never returned.

About a month after the strike was called, eleven mills signed the agreement with the union, placing 1200 people back at work. This gave new encouragement to the strikers.

One day as several pickets were leaving a struck shop, an

automobile pulled up to the curb, and a lady said, "Where are you going?" One of the fellows said, "To the Labor Lyceum to a strike meeting." The lady said, "I am the wife of your boss, and I have heard the manufacturers' side of the story and would like to hear yours." One of these boys was chairman of the shop. He told her why we had struck. After hearing this, she said, "I would like to attend one of these meetings." The fellows said, "We will have to ask the officials of the union first." She invited them into the car, and drove them to the Union Hall where she was given permission to attend the meeting. After the meeting, she congratulated the chairman, and said, "I will do all I can to persuade the firm to sign the agreement with the union. I will never believe the radical stories that are told of strikers as they are a very peaceful and well mannered group of girls and fellows." It was not long after this that this firm did sign the agreement.

The A. shop was one of the biggest mills, and employed about 2000 people. There were only about three or four who came out the first day. Most of these workers were foreigners and afraid to strike. The boss had told them if they struck he would have them deported, as it was through him that they had come to this country. Not knowing any better, they believe him.

The union rented a house opposite the mill, and opened a branch office, to encourage the workers to join the strike. Some of our German speaking members held secret meetings with some of those workers, and explained in their own language what the strike was about. The meetings were held secretly for about one month when the boss found out about one. He sent spies to watch the meeting. There were about a hundred there. The next morning when they went to work, nine men were fired for attending this meeting.

When the word was passed around that these men had been fired, the other men and girls walked out. As they left their machines, they were not allowed to speak to anyone, but escorted straight to the elevator by one of the cops in plain clothes. Quite a few came out on strike.

There were not enough strikers from this mill for picketing. At the strike meeting, we had to ask for volunteer pickets. So eager were the strikers to show this manufacturer we wanted his workers to join us, that when we asked for pickets almost the whole meeting volunteered.

The next day we had a mass picket at this shop, and we thought all the cops in the city were on duty there. We could hardly get near the place for cops. Traffic was tied up on three streets. Trolleys were stopped, and could go no further for the congestion. For all the protection the scabs had, they were ashamed to come out to go home.

In a few days this shop got an injunction against the union and we were allowed only ten pickets. After the hearing of the injunction, the judge handed down a permanent injunction against the union whereby we could not picket within five blocks of the shop, nor could we try to organize nor distribute pamphlets of any kind. We were also instructed to move our branch office.

This strike aroused so much attention that an appeal was sent to the mayor to see what he could do to try to bring it to a favorable end. This led to the mayor's Fact Finding Committee. Facts were submitted by our union and the non-union employers to this committee.

After the facts were submitted, the committee urged the union to call off the strike, and strongly urged the non-union employers to cooperate with the employees and reinstate as many as possible. Employers were also urged to engage a competent staff to guide them in personnel, policies and industrial relations. This report did not do anything for the strikers.

The strike lasted about six months, when it was called off by the union. At the end of that period, twenty-one shops had signed the agreement with the union which brought about 2100 new members into the union.

THE READING PICKET LINE

It was in September, 1931, when the New Jersey, New York, and New England hosiery mills were affected by an insurgent strike. When the manufacturers announced the new low rates, the workers quit their jobs and struck to combat the drastic wage cut, which amounted from 35 to 45 per cent on various operations. Beside the organized shops, several non-union shops walked out in sympathy that created a very effective feeling towards the development of organization.

But the most striking and interesting feature that ever developed in the life of the American Labor Movement, was the Reading drive. This was attempted by the strikers of the three districts to induce a walk out in the Reading mills against the extreme wage cuts in the hosiery industry in the last few years.

Various and numerous approaches and attempts had been made for a number of years to teach Reading what organization would mean in the hosiery industry, and the power it would give in combating different ills imposed on the workers. But still there seemed to be some fear that prevented the workers from cooperating with other workers, who were trying their utmost to stabilize the hosiery industry and equalize conditions.

As a new means to induce the Berkshire employees to a walk out, the three districts decided to campaign and influence the workers with a tremendous effort. The Berkshire is the largest mill in the country and has always been non-union.

Among the 5,000 insurgent strikers, about 3,000 migrated to Reading from the New Jersey, New York, and New England states either in private cars or buses. Arriving at Reading and gathering on the Socialist Picnic grounds about 4:30 A. M., they made a very interesting picture. Hundreds of cars came driving on the grounds with several buses from the three districts, and formed a picture of a little colony surrounded by a wall of cars. At 6 A. M., every member of this colony group was on the job to picket the Berkshire mill about five miles away from the picnic grounds. Arriving at the mill gates, all pickets were formed in lines, about 1500 in number. These pickets walked up and down the street continually, very peacefully trying to approach the workers in the mills. While among many workers there seemed to be a great deal of sympathy, there was also a fear that kept them from cooperating.

For almost a week, the huge picket line was maintained at the Berkshire mills, increasing in number the second and third days until there were between 2,500 and 3,000 pickets carrying on a demonstration. So peaceful were they carrying on the demonstration

that there was no police interference until the fifth day, when the
state police interfered and limited the number of pickets on duty.

This demonstration did make a wonderful impression on the
employees, and at times it seemed that they would walk out. The
drive was not successful, although the Berkshire employees did become aware of the strength of our organized ranks, and our desire
to help them.

MY EXPERIENCE IN THE LABOR MOVEMENT

When the organizer from the Full Fashioned Hosiery Workers' Union started to organize the workers in the mill in which I worked, he got the boys first. Then they got some girls interested. These girls in turn talked to others in their departments. One girl was discharged because of union activities. After the discharging of this girl, she would stand out in front of the mill with the organizers, handing out the Hosiery Workers' Magazine and cards with the dates and places of the meetings on them.

I was afraid to take any of the papers for fear the boss would see me. Finally, I began taking the papers and reading them after I got home. In a few weeks I began taking the papers into the mill to read during lunch hour. One day the foreman told me not to let the boss see me with them. That made me want to find out more. I asked one of the knitter's wives if she had been to any meetings with her husband. She said she had and asked me to go to one. I persuaded a few girls in my department to go with me to find out what they were for. We joined the union that night. The next day other girls, eager to know what we found out, insisted on being taken to a meeting. They also joined the union.

The time came for action. A shop committee was chosen to ask the boss for recognition of our union. He flatly refused, thinking he could get us to sign our names to an agreement known as a company union. He was disappointed in this undertaking as no one would sign it.

This attitude on the part of the management called for an election to determine representatives of our own choosing for collective bargaining. Mr. James Dewey, representative of the National Labor Board, was sent to conduct the voting.

We were not allowed to vote until working hours were over (after 4:00 P. M.). At 3:00 the company called a meeting, informing us that they objected to the vote, and saying we might as well accept their committee for representatives in collective bargaining, because since there was not any company union nor opponent the vote would be illegal. The results, however, were seven to one in favor of the Hosiery Workers' Union.

After six months of waiting for something to move in our direction, a strike vote was taken and a strike called for April 6. There were three weeks of peaceful picketing and the management put a notice on the doors that the mill had ceased operations. The pickets were then moved to an affiliated mill, where their union had also gone out on strike.

At this time extra police were put on duty, and about twenty-five thugs were brought in to take scabs to and from work. These thugs caused much trouble. Every night there was a clash between them and strikers. A lot of cars were damaged and torn up. One day a gang of strikers was standing on an impartial corner when four of the thugs appeared, displaying guns, and told them to move on.

Union officials and strikers appealed to the mayor, for some kind of protection against these law breakers. The mayor called them down, and found they had permits to carry guns signed by a constable whose term of office as such had expired, but who had been hired by the company to sign the permits for its strike breakers.

When those thugs departed, the company purchased four Greyhound busses at a cost of $40,000. The busses, used to haul scabs, were escorted by two police cars carrying eight policemen.

From this again came conflicts between scabs and strikers. One day I happened to be in one of them with two girls. The scabs dragged me into a grocery store and held me on the floor until someone called the police. I was arrested for assault and battery and disorderly conduct. My hearing was set for the next day. At the entrance to the court room, I was informed by the lawyer that the defendants were demanding trial, and he consented with the intention of appealing the case if I got a sentence. The scabs had fourteen witnesses, but were only allowed to use two, as the only one I had was the arresting officer who, upon being questioned as to my conduct when he arrested me, said that I was being held on the floor by the hair and hands, unable to move. I got $1 and costs ($11), and a thirty day jail sentence. My lawyer appealed the case, and it was thrown out after thirty days.

Every evening about 5:00, the strikers and sympathizers would line up across the street from the mill and watch the busses as they drove out of the alley with the scabs. One evening there were several rocks thrown at the buss by some one, and the police started shooting into the crowd.

The scabs swore warrants for the arrest of several strikers. Our organizer and the financial secretary of the international organization were arrested on a charge of inciting to riot. They were released after being put under bond to keep the peace. The company then got an injunction prohibiting us from going down the street between the buildings, and keeping us from picketing the mill. The union officials turned around and got an injunction against the chief of police who appealed it to the State Supreme Court, and the judge of the court lifted both injunctions.

The strike situation was taken up for a hearing by the National Labor Board. They decided that the majority vote must rule for one year, ignoring our protest. An agreement was drawn up which did not give the strikers much voice, but they accepted it, as the National Labor Board was sending a conciliator to take up the discrimination cases. Two weeks later an agreement was reached for our mill. We did not get recognition of the union, but we did get recognition of the shop committee, and reinstatement of all strikers in their former jobs.

STRIKE

The plant was closed down May 11 for overhauling the machinery and then it was opened up again in July. They let everybody work
two days. The work had been stretched-out. I filled fifty-two bat-
teries before May; I had to fill seventy-two in July. The union had
a meeting and decided to strike against the stretch-out.

The strike was called July 23. The men formed picket lines
around the mill. One afternoon late in August, seven strange men
came to the mill office and demanded that all the picketing men get
off the mill grounds. The men cursed the women, and after they found
out that the union people were not doing any harm, they went to the
hotel for the night. The union people kept the picket lines all the
next day until 5:00 P. M. That afternoon guards were sent down to
the mill to take charge. They made all the union people cross the
road to form the picket lines. They could not get any closer to the
mill than the road.

One night before Christmas, most all the people were off
the village. The scabs made up a mob of men, dressed them like Ku
Klux and marched over the village carrying burning crosses. They
put one up at the house of the president of the local union. He
would kick it down as fast as they put it up. They marched on to
the secretary's house still carrying burning crosses.

The mill was started the first of September with non-union
help. They did not post a notice telling that the mill was going to
start up. But the union people went to the office and applied for
jobs and the manager said that he would send for them to come to
work. He did send for one or two, but about 250 people were left
without jobs.

When the N.R.A. was ruled unconstitutional, our case was
thrown out of court. Then the company sent notices out to the
people asking them to vacate the houses at once.

A DAY IN JAIL

It was the seventh day of our strike. I reported as usual for picket duty in front of the factory. For a while all was quiet. Suddenly I noticed a girl coming toward the factory in a great hurry with a fresh expression on her face. I thought to myself, "She sure looks as though she is going into work." I stopped her. "Where are you going in such a rush?"

"I have lost a week's work and pay on account of your foolish strike. Because you've lost your own job you want me to lose mine," she cried in a sharp angry voice.

I tried to reason with her by telling her that I was striking for the protection of her job and wages as well as mine.

"Keep moving, girl!" I turned around and saw a husky cop pointing at me with his club. As I did not move, he pushed me off the side walk.

I got angry. "You have nerve to push me around like this. I'm a tax payer and help pay your wages," I yelled.

"So you're a fresh kid, huh? I'll show you!" He called the patrol wagon and shoved me in. All the other pickets surrounded me; some of them got in the patrol wagon with me. They did not want me to go alone.

They crowded all fifteen of us in two cells in the police station. I was shocked at the first sight of the cell. It had no windows; the only light we had was through the bars of the door. The walls and floor were dirty, and there was an open toilet in one corner of the cell exposed to the view of any one who passed the cell. The only other furniture consisted of two boards fastened to the walls for seats. Cobwebs and scribbling on the walls were the decorations. I sat for a full hour reading the scribbling. There was plenty of time. We had to wait five hours before the magistrate arrived. We were hungry, too, and although we called the matron to tell her we wanted something to eat, she paid no attention to us.

We were growing more and more disgusted, but no one thought of offering to pay a fine. We were proud to stick by our cause. We kept telling one another that we would stick together, no matter how hard it was. Just then the matron appeared. It seemed strange to see her unlock the door. She called my name and told me to follow her. In the hall I saw our lawyer. I almost screamed with joy.

We went to the magistrate. "What has she done?" the magistrate asked.

I turned to our lawyer and said, "Since when is talking to a girl on the side walk a crime?"

The magistrate laughed, "If you promise not to go on the picket line again, you will be released right away." I promised I would call off the strike to do him a favor. Of course we were back on the picket line the very next morning.

MY FIRST EXPERIENCE IN JAIL

On the third day of our strike, we decided to have a mass picket line in order to make the strike more effective. I was on the committee to take care of the picket line and received instructions to go to the union office and ask for the pickets.

After presenting our situation, I was told by our organizer that everything possible would be done. Later in the afternoon a few strikers and I went to the picket line.

The first thing I saw when we arrived was a large mob of people who were being pushed around by the police. I did not know what it was all about as it was my first experience on a picket line. With great difficulty I worked my way through the crowd. Suddenly I heard a voice, "Get her - that's the one!" Before I had a chance to look around, I was grabbed by a great big policeman who was saying, "Come on, you are going for a nice ride!" I recall having three feelings all at the same time: I was embarrassed, angry and frightened. The crowd however was cheering me. "Don't be afraid. You will not be there more than an hour!" I can not say that I was very enthusiastic about it, however, and tried to resist. I do not know how but I soon found myself in a cage. For a while I was lost. I did not know whether to stand or sit, cry or laugh. It was not long, however, before I had company; five more girls were thrown in with me.

After riding twenty minutes (it seemed like as many hours), we were unloaded at a police station. For two hours they questioned us as though we were some terrible criminals. When it was finally over, I wondered what would come next. I thought we would be told to go home, but no. We were taken for another ride, this time to a jail. There they asked more questions, and not only that, they searched us. We asked why we had to be searched. The answer was, "Well, you may have some weapons with which you may hurt yourselves."

What next? I heard a voice, "Follow me." We followed and found ourselves in a cell. That was too much for me. I could not help but burst into tears for the place looked horrid to me. The only thing I could see was a toilet and two benches covered with dirty blankets. The blankets were so dirty that we did not dare to sit on them. In the next cell was a woman of about thirty, leaning against the cell wall and staring at us with a pitifully blank and hopeless expression on her aging face. She could have been playing the part of dope fiend in the movies, but this was grim reality.

We stayed in that terrible place for a half hour or so and then were told, "Well, you have been bailed out, so you may go home." I hurried home, glad to put the experience behind me, but I can never forget the way we were rounded up and herded into jail like criminals, for the "crime" of fighting for our existence.

ALL IN A STRIKER'S DAY

At 2:00 in the afternoon of a very warm, sultry May day, about 300 hosiery strikers surged up a street only one half square from the main millgate. They were young men and young women, who had walked the picket line at least eighteen hours out of every day since the strike had started, six weeks before. Tired, haggard faces, unshaven faces, eyes that were heavy and red for want of sleep and rest. Shoulders that were stooped from working long hours in the factory when they should still have been outside playing. Yes, they were young, but one could feel the determined air and the tenseness of the whole group.

The bus, or ratcage so called because it hauled the scabs to and from work and was always guarded by police, and a squad car passed. It was directly in front of my home, when a young man, who had formerly worked in the mill, threw a rock through the side window of the bus.

It stopped at once. Five big, burly, red faced cops jumped out of the bus. The one in front jerked his gun out of the holster and yelled, "Kill him! damm him! kill him!"

He shot wildly through the crowd. Three shots hit the garage in the back yard. Had they hit the boys that were running through the yard, these lads would have been killed instantly.

My two brothers, one thirteen years old, the other fifteen years old, and my baby sister, who is eleven years old, were playing in the backyard, when those bullets went whizzing by.

One shot barely missed my eighteen year old sister, also a striker, who was standing in the side yard. Her nerves, which had never been good and were worse after six weeks on the picket line, gave way and she fainted. Immediately the crowd went wild, with anger and excitement.

"Is she hurt?"

"Come on, boys, they've hurt her!"

"Let's show 'em how to fight. To hell with their guns and clubs!"

"Take him! His number is five-forty-eight!"

"We'll show 'em how to shoot young school kids and girls!"

Tiredness and sleepiness had vanished. One thought, one

idea, swayed the angry, defiant young strikers.

"Wait, gang, one minute please. She isn't shot. Just the shock. Please be quiet, she can't stand the noise."

The cops were not so brave now. They were pleading with the mob to dispense instead of bull-dozing with their guns and clubs.

A striker came around the house carrying my baby sister, who was crying and begging for Sis.

"Is she hurt?"

"Please, let's take these damn kid killers!"

"Gang, won't you please be quiet. You haven't a chance against armed cops. The kids aren't hurt, so please quiet down. They can't stand any more. If for no other reason, for their sake, stop this riot."

"We will if these lousy damn cops will leave."

They were only too glad to go.

Quiet reigned again. The strikers, loyal to the last one, gathered around my mother.

"May we help?"

"Isn't there anything we can do for you and the kids?"

"Do you want us to guard the house tonight?"

"Wouldn't you feel better if one or two of us stayed with you tonight?"

"No, boys, I think quiet and peace will help us more right now. I will call you if we need anything."

So they silently marched back to the endless walking of the picket line to end one more day of the strike.

UNDER CONTROL

It was in the very early morning and we had been told to be out on the picket line. The sky was a murky grey. The weather was raw and biting. We stood in front of a tall dirty white building in the heart of the city. The streets were deserted except for one or two early birds on their way to work.

We walked up and down jumping now and then to keep from freezing. A thrill ran up and down my spine. I was waiting, for what, I did not know.

We were used to being on the picket line but this one was something different. This was a racketeer shop, and it had a reputation. The shop had been watched by a special committee whose orders were to spot workers so we could approach them. This work had been carried on for a long time. Now we were there and our job ahead of us. The tension was strong for we were a measly twenty as compared to the 400 employed there.

People started to approach us. Would they enter the building or would they go on? A woman was entering. Two girls followed her. When they spoke to her, she snapped back at them, "Leave me alone. I'll have nothing to do with you. I am not interested. Get out of here!" Our girls tried to continue the conversation but she was too close to the elevator so they had to let her go.

Suddenly one of our group called out, "Here are some more." We moved on masse toward the approaching women, surrounded them and started to talk to them. They objected and refused to listen. "Union, hell! We're satisfied. We don't need a union. Give you our money? I'll say not." I was trying to talk to a tall woman but she just laughed at me in a sneering manner. My blood boiled. Oh, control! Dear control!

Another in the group called us foreigners and reds. We had closed in and formed quite a crowd around these four girls. Then suddenly one called out, "Hey, there, Jerry, get these pests away," and as she said this she struck the nearest one to her. The others followed her example, and we were fighting. Blow after blow was exchanged. I slapped and scratched. I found a hat in my hand, threw it away, closed my fist and socked hard. I could hear the thud of other blows around me. A little further off I could see the others fighting. The group had loosened into individual battles. People were coming, too many people. I heard a whistle somewhere, took a last look around at the scene and ran. So did the others. I dodged into a restaurant, hurried to the ladies' room and tidied up. When I came out, all was excitement but no one seemed to know what had happened. I asked a cop and he said, "Just another union brawl, lady. That's all. Everything is under control."

A PICKET LINE

I reached the strike headquarters where I found myself greeted by many workers whose faces showed lack of sleep, but glowed with enthusiasm. Everyone was restlessly wondering what another two-day battle would bring. The only desire of many hundreds of workers was to stop that one particular mill where the boss had brought in strike breakers.

At last, all packed in trucks and singing cheerfully, wo set off. In a short time we were there, greeted by many hundreds of workers who had already come out on the picket line. It seemed that not only our own ranks were filled with enthusiasm, but even the inhabitants of the neighboring houses greeted us with strong smiles of solidarity. My, what a pessimist I was to have thought that our industry could not be strongly organized in a short time!

Songs of labor rang from different directions. "Hold the Fort for We are Coming" came from one side, while on the other rang the words of "Solidarity Forever" and "The Union Makes Us Strong." The police seemed almost helpless as hundreds of workers gathered at an entrance where the machines bringing the scabs came to a stop. Again the voices of workers rang forth as a thunder with cheers and songs.

But a sudden change took place as police mounted on horses came on, breaking up our line with their clubs. Their faces were embittered, and they turned at us with their shields as though we were animals. Their eyes showed lack of human understanding. Their mouths were drawn tight. They were determined to break our ranks. Their clubs as they were thrown around, and the horses as they stepped on us, turned our singing voices into screams of pain. We were running from one end to another. Where? No one knew. The doors of the neighboring homes were opened to save us from the horses hoofs.

Alleys, porches, and yards are still flitting before my eyes. The battle continuing for a couple of hours left us exhausted. How many arrests? How many hurt? How many beaten up? These were my thoughts as I walked the streets. Several detectives with brutal expressions in their eyes followed us for several blocks. What sort of crime have we committed? Have we no right to demand a human standard of living? Yet Section 7a entered my mind: the right to organize! But do not be in your bosses' way.......

When I reached the headquarters, I knew already from the faces of my fellow workers that the attempt of the bosses and their tools to break our ranks had succeeded. But are they broken forever? No! Has this battle broke our spirit and solidarity? Again I say, no! This bloody picket line will remain in the memories of the workers in our industry as an inspiration in the future struggle for a final victory.

BS&AU
12646

Women in America

FROM COLONIAL TIMES TO THE 20TH CENTURY

An Arno Press Collection

Andrews, John B. and W. D. P. Bliss. **History of Women in Trade Unions** (*Report on Conditions of Woman and Child Wage-Earners in the United States,* Vol. X; 61st Congress, 2nd Session, Senate Document No. 645). 1911

Anthony, Susan B. **An Account of the Proceedings on the Trial of Susan B. Anthony, on the Charge of Illegal Voting at the Presidential Election in November, 1872,** and on the Trial of Beverly W. Jones, Edwin T. Marsh and William B. Hall, the Inspectors of Election by Whom her Vote was Received. 1874

The Autobiography of a Happy Woman. 1915

Ayer, Harriet Hubbard. **Harriet Hubbard Ayer's Book:** A Complete and Authentic Treatise on the Laws of Health and Beauty. 1902

Barrett, Kate Waller. **Some Practical Suggestions on the Conduct of a Rescue Home.** *Including* **Life of Dr. Kate Waller Barrett** (Reprinted from *Fifty Years' Work With Girls* by Otto Wilson). [1903]

Bates, Mrs. D. B. **Incidents on Land and Water;** Or, Four Years on the Pacific Coast. 1858

Blumenthal, Walter Hart. **Women Camp Followers of the American Revolution.** 1952

Boothe, Viva B., editor. **Women in the Modern World** (*The Annals of the American Academy of Political and Social Science,* Vol. CXLIII, May 1929). 1929

Bowne, Eliza Southgate. **A Girl's Life Eighty Years Ago:** Selections from the Letters of Eliza Southgate Bowne. 1888

Brooks, Geraldine. **Dames and Daughters of Colonial Days.** 1900

Carola Woerishoffer: Her Life and Work. 1912

Clement, J[esse], editor. **Noble Deeds of American Women;** With Biographical Sketches of Some of the More Prominent. 1851

Crow, Martha Foote. **The American Country Girl.** 1915

De Leon, T[homas] C. **Belles, Beaux and Brains of the 60's.**
1909

de Wolfe, Elsie (Lady Mendl). **After All.** 1935

Dix, Dorothy (Elizabeth Meriwether Gilmer). **How to Win and
Hold a Husband.** 1939

Donovan, Frances R. **The Saleslady.** 1929

Donovan, Frances R. **The Schoolma'am.** 1938

Donovan, Frances R. **The Woman Who Waits.** 1920

Eagle, Mary Kavanaugh Oldham, editor. **The Congress of
Women,** Held in the Woman's Building, World's Columbian
Exposition, Chicago, U.S.A., 1893. 1894

Ellet, Elizabeth F. **The Eminent and Heroic Women of America.**
1873

Ellis, Anne. **The Life of an Ordinary Woman.** 1929

[Farrar, Eliza W. R.] **The Young Lady's Friend.** By a Lady.
1836

Filene, Catherine, editor. **Careers for Women.** 1920

Finley, Ruth E. **The Lady of Godey's:** Sarah Josepha Hale. 1931
Fragments of Autobiography. 1974

Frost, John. **Pioneer Mothers of the West;** Or, Daring and
Heroic Deeds of American Women. 1869

[Gilman], Charlotte Perkins Stetson. **In This Our World.** 1899

Goldberg, Jacob A. and Rosamond W. Goldberg. **Girls on the
City Streets:** A Study of 1400 Cases of Rape. 1935

Grace H. Dodge: Her Life and Work. 1974

Greenbie, Marjorie Barstow. **My Dear Lady:** The Story of Anna
Ella Carroll, the "Great Unrecognized Member of Lincoln's
Cabinet." 1940

Hourwich, Andria Taylor and Gladys L. Palmer, editors. **I Am
a Woman Worker:** A Scrapbook of Autobiographies. 1936

Howe, M[ark] A. De Wolfe. **Memories of a Hostess:**
A Chronicle of Friendships Drawn Chiefly from the Diaries of
Mrs. James T. Fields. 1922

Irwin, Inez Haynes. **Angels and Amazons:** A Hundred Years of
American Women. 1934

Laughlin, Clara E. **The Work-a-Day Girl:** A Study of Some
Present-Day Conditions. 1913

Lewis, Dio. **Our Girls.** 1871

Liberating the Home. 1974

Livermore, Mary A. **The Story of My Life; Or, The Sunshine
and Shadow of Seventy Years . . . To Which is Added Six
of Her Most Popular Lectures. 1899

Lives to Remember. 1974

Lobsenz, Johanna. **The Older Woman in Industry.** 1929

MacLean, Annie Marion. **Wage-Earning Women.** 1910

Meginness, John F. **Biography of Frances Slocum, the Lost
Sister of Wyoming:** A Complete Narrative of her Captivity of
Wanderings Among the Indians. 1891

Nathan, Maud. **Once Upon a Time and Today.** 1933

[Packard, Elizabeth Parsons Ware]. **Great Disclosure of
Spiritual Wickedness!!** In High Places. With an Appeal to the
Government to Protect the Inalienable Rights of Married Women.
1865

Parsons, Alice Beal. **Woman's Dilemma.** 1926

Parton, James, et al. **Eminent Women of the Age:** Being
Narratives of the Lives and Deeds of the Most Prominent
Women of the Present Generation. 1869

Paton, Lucy Allen. **Elizabeth Cary Agassiz:** A Biography. 1919

Rayne, M[artha] L[ouise]. **What Can a Woman Do;** Or, Her
Position in the Business and Literary World. 1893

Richmond, Mary E. and Fred S. Hall. **A Study of Nine Hundred
and Eighty-Five Widows Known to Certain Charity Organization
Societies in 1910.** 1913

Ross, Ishbel. **Ladies of the Press:** The Story of Women in
Journalism by an Insider. 1936

Sex and Equality. 1974

Snyder, Charles McCool. **Dr. Mary Walker:** The Little Lady in
Pants. 1962

Stow, Mrs. J. W. **Probate Confiscation:** Unjust Laws Which
Govern Woman. 1878

Sumner, Helen L. **History of Women in Industry in the United**

States (*Report on Conditions of Woman and Child Wage-Earners in the United States,* Vol. IX; 61st Congress, 2nd Session, Senate Document No. 645). 1910

[Vorse, Mary H.] **Autobiography of an Elderly Woman.** 1911

Washburn, Charles. **Come into My Parlor:** A Biography of the Aristocratic Everleigh Sisters of Chicago. 1936

Women of Lowell. 1974

Woolson, Abba Gould. **Dress-Reform:** A Series of Lectures Delivered in Boston on Dress as it Affects the Health of Women. 1874

Working Girls of Cincinnati. 1974